Cascadia

Beyond the bioregion...

The Noocracy

Chapters:

Incentive for a nation

Many nations have revolted for one reason or another through history. We live in a society where clothing lines are producing not only fake holes in the knee but the look of the anarchist. What is a revolution to you? What would be the best type of revolution for mankind to have? I often think this to myself. A revolution of the mind! It must be... What kind of a World will we live in if we don't prioritize wisdom and intelligence? You have to think what it is that people have failed to understand when you zoom out and look at the grand scheme of things through the centuries. I find one common thread that runs through every civilization and it is men have metaphorically pressed the face of his brother into the ground with the boot of authority. Mankind reeks of dehumanization from Kings conducting compulsive beheadings to that of the iconic electric chair. We have used our authority to strike fear into those around us who would dare go against our multitude of regulations and mandates. At what point do we take a stand? For the nation with the most incarceration I was also born into this mantra of liberty and freedom. It is in the songs we sing that we are supposed to let freedom ring from sea to shining sea. There is a sort of paradox afoot where one after a certain bit enlightened realizes that you can't have both a vast prison system and freedom in the same breath. Why have we been dealt this hand? Has no one noticed that prison is merely government sanctioned torture? Man has put his fellow man in a cage like something worse than an animal under the guise of justice for generations. Centuries we have done this and called it good. It is supposed to be the good of humanity. Why is it then that we reward a police dog instead of punishing it? The same logic is simply not applied to human beings. I find it interesting the Babemba tribe would gather the village around and tell someone all the good deeds they've done to humiliate someone who had done something bad. What is bad? For ages we have co-opted the nature of good and bad and built our ethics at the time and embedded them into the government from the walks of many cultures and religions. Is freedom important when faced with the overwhelming zeitgeist of masses? What about basic rights? As a radio host I found it wild that the FCC could fine a collage station over 20 thousand dollars for swearing on the air. Under what kind of encroaching authority has this anti-swearing politically correct Medusa come from? The same type of authority that has so cleverly galvanized a fee and a fine into every facet of life... The government. With seemingly unlimited spending the US has used fear to prop up a myriad of things. A currency based on debt that ironically has the faces of former presidents who would be rolling in their graves in 1913. A time when corporations suddenly had the rights of a citizen and government strangely became in bed with the corn industry. This is when the Idiocracy in America really began. How is it rational for the government to pay off farmers so they will grow corn, corn and more corn? Our farming was meant to yield a diverse dichotomy of different types of crops. This diversity is integral to our sustainability and survival as a species. Irrigation in the west was our 1st true stage of civilization. The Romans would of never become as great if they had not invented the Aqueduct. You can see America and it's corn slowly dry the further you drive east. I noticed in the east their corn was scorched from lacking that 1st stage and this was just considered normal. If I were to go east and preach about irrigation would the people of the Bible belts listen? There is a phenomenon that pops up when presenting people with new information they aren't used to hearing. It is called Cognitive Dissonance. In a meme it says: "Sometimes people hold a core belief that is very strong. When they are presented with evidence that works against that belief, the new evidence cannot be accepted. It would create a feeling that is extremely uncomfortable called Cognitive Dissonance. And because it is so important to protect said core belief, they will rationalize, ignore and even destroy anything that doesn't fit with that core belief." Parting from the topic of corn and how it can be manipulated to cause sterility and organ failure something the average person cannot fathom at the dinner table, it most often occurs when people hold the core belief that the Justice system is good. It is certainly not good when it allows execution! Well that would be new information contrary to the prevailing core belief that execution for a horrible crime is not only tolerable but ethical. In contrast as the World's smartest man or merely the 1st person to understand basic rights they would be wrong to continue down the same road. America was supposed to be different! When Thomas Jefferson wrote the declaration of independence in 1776 it had a nice ring to it but the average person even at the time could not contemplate this light at the end would manifest it's self into Cascadia. If people ask me why I left the union from the US I will talk about our unalienable right to life above and before everything. Certainly if the US had been upholding our unalienable right to life execution would no longer be allowed by the government! Certainly it's police would understand that the government doesn't actually have the authority to blow your brains out! You see that would be violating your unalienable right to life! How is it that after 241 years of America trying to sound noble we still have a country that is like so many in the past? Nobody understood Jefferson the wisest man of his day. Only until now does anyone!   And there is the problem. The Noocracy as described by Plato must exist to educate the public what basic rights are. Jefferson said "Educate and inform the whole mass of the people... They are the only sure reliance for the preservation of our liberty." Certainly Jefferson was ahead of his time. If only the people listened to Nikola Tesla the smartest man of his day we would have wireless electricity instead of this high voltage web of death over our heads. We have had 100 years of flight and we are still on the ground. Freedom starts in the mind. Did the government make you believe that rights are alienable?   Free your mind. The prevailing ethics have not changed to this day. We have allowed the worst side of human nature, the vindictive side that seeks revenge a voice in justice. This was and will always be a grave mistake. Parting from the British at least they knew to put their murderers on a far off Island like Australia. In that regard they were more civilized. Such a revelation embarrasses America and secessionist movements like the Cascadian movement embrace all that was good in the country during this time. Rather than rise like the south before the civil war we in the west want to remind America of its true foundation born in equality and basic rights.

Please read this passage of the declaration of independence once again:

We hold these truths to be self-evident, that all men are created equal, that they are endowed by their Creator with certain unalienable Rights, that among these are Life, Liberty and the pursuit of Happiness. — That to secure these rights,

Governments are instituted among Men, deriving their just powers from the consent of the governed, — That whenever any Form of Government becomes destructive of these ends, it is the Right of the People to alter or to abolish it, and to institute new Government, laying its foundation on such principles and organizing its powers in such form, as to them shall seem most likely to effect their Safety and Happiness.

It says if the US it's self fails to understand our rights we have a right to alter or abolish it and put in place a new government.

This is the Cognitive Dissonance I am talking about that it seems so unreasonable that there could possibly be this big of a blunder where every government authority from the Supreme Court, to governors to presidents would fail to understand basic rights. Instead the prevailing idea is that murder is ok if the government does it. This means that no jury who convicted a person to death has understood. If the average person in the majority fails to understand the most basic right to life we are in grave danger of total dehumanization. We have seen such dehumanization already. Originally called "The Negro Project" I banned Planned Parenthood for aborting babies and selling body parts on the black market. If America's largest march in history the pink hat march shows the number of people who support Planned Parenthood regardless we have a colossal failure in understanding. The supreme court is supposed to understand basic rights before Roe Vs Wade happens. This shows you why I wouldn't want a democratic vote. The majority doesn't understand murder is a violation of our rights. Indoctrinated with Hollywood shoot em ups we grew up thinking guns are the law and it's the Wild West. So can Jay Inslee represent me if he doesn't yet understand the right to life? No he cannot. None of these representatives elected or running seem to understand. An Idiocracy is when the public and politicians fail to care for public health and safety in the face of a serious hazard for over a decade. An example of this can be found when Gerald Cox convinced politicians that an illegal waste from the aluminum industry was good for bones and teeth! Someone said a neurotoxin commonly used to kill roaches and rats was just fine and dandy for putting in the municipal water supply that we drink back in 1937. Why has no one questioned it for 80 years? Because people often do not think for themselves and will be happy to buy any idea that has a one liner of proverbial scientific data. They want to still sound smart so they will argue that rat poison is actually good for you in low enough doses. At some point a volunteer who is the Noocracy steps forward and attempts to tell the public that they have been wrong about many things for years.

The Noocracy attempts to provide common sense under a thundering cloud of mockery and ridicule. Something as simple as the idea that you cannot make the sick get better in the hospital while malnourishing them with microwaved food is overlooked as crazy. You can tell your parents all about how microwaved food causes brain damage but they have used the machine too long to listen to reason. Often in an Idiocracy the garbage only piles higher until problems are dealt with at the last minute ending in a climatic garbage avalanche or Fukushima like disaster. World War III may be one of those things that humanity keeps trying to sweep under the rug till it's too late. Sometimes consider that extraterrestrials may save the planet from a future we are unware of during an incident that seems meaningless like the anomaly we saw blowing up a Facebook satellite during a Falcon 9 Space X rocket launch. We are left to wonder. Perhaps they blew it up mistaking it for an ICBM. Are aliens that dumb? Perhaps it is so I will talk about it in this book and awaken you to the idea that this is going on, on a regular basis. Who will stop the US from going too far after 9-11? We have the prospect of another rouge nation after World War 2 behaving in a similar fashion under the guise of fighting terrorism when the US smashes a sovereign nation like Libya. Smashing any nation that doesn't like to use the American petro dollar seems to be the trend. I find nothing wrong with the fact that Gadhafi wanted to use the gold standard to lift his country. Gold has been used since the times of Egypt but it exposes another irrational behavior. Why? It makes no rational sense for gold to have such value. Come to the realization that mankind does things like this over long periods of time putting value on strange things it shouldn't. What if the process of looking for gold puts mercury into the river? What if our lust for diamonds is fueling underground arms trade and terrorism in another country? There is that disconnect in America where Diamonds are forever and are never seen as the blood Diamonds they really are. When the military leadership of America seems to care more about the paranoia of Israel than its own national security the Noocracy is looking not only to build a new nation but to build a World ARMY where rouge nations are no longer allowed to parade about the globe flattening and framing sovereign nations with chemical weapons. As World general I may warn that it is irresponsible for the US to give billions in arms to Saudi Arabia when they are suspected already of Nuking Yemen during the Obama administration. I may warn of many things but who listens to the World's smartest man? It is the egocentric who are psycho enough to put their own national agenda before international stability. It is the egocentric who have a new found passion and pride for having the bomb. Einstein who wished he was a watchmaker and warned us about the future misuse of nuclear weapons but did the World listen to him? No. When you give a monkey a machine gun he shoots it at people and puts it above his head in triumph. America has blood on its hands. It has something worse than blood. There is something worse than burning people at the stake and making necklaces out of their ears. America's weapons are born out of a great cruelty like Asian Orange. That will hang a heavy cloud over its head for generations. Should Cascadia a new nation intending to lead the World in environmentalism become cannon fodder from bad blood over the Korean War? Do you expect the Seattle Seahawks to continue to stand for the national anthem of the former government when we have our own anthem?

3 years after leaving the union you would think someone might of heard it by now over the ocean of spam. One might expect this that the media will remain American and hide any secessionist movement as a means of saving it's self from the embarrassment. To what extent will America go to hide its ugly side. There certainly is one. It is the same side of America that hides its conquest of the middle east under the wing of fighting terror pushing while The project for a greater Israel and its nation state seek expansion. Unconditionally each president for the last few decades seems to care more about talking in front of AIPAC than the American people. Why does the US "stand with Israel" when they show the true face of dehumanization in their oppression of the Palestinians? Don't we condemn the treatment of the Jews during the Holocaust? At the end of the day we turn a blind eye to human suffering and wave a flag as if it is justified in our patriotism. How can we stand idle when internationally banned weapons like white phosphorus are used

and women and children are bullied by militants? The America I know wouldn't of jumped to conclusions after 9-11 and wouldn't of devastated an entire region of the globe with Depleted Uranium munitions. This is the behavior as we saw that contaminated Falluja indefinitely for generations. An umbrella of future deformed children will be born there. Yes DU is a superior munition on the battle field heavier than lead but at what cost? It is no different than the humanitarian crisis that still exists today from Agent Orange. Children are born mutated. This mutation lasts for generations. How can the US expect zero repercussions from this type of behavior? The children of our own troops are born without arms from the handling of DU munitions on the battlefield. The America I know is more honorable and is beholding to a noninterventionist foreign policy. Half of its history consists of having one. Hidden national agendas and greed set the stage. The erosion from its previous state has confused and bewildered an unwitting population of flag wavers. America hasn't always been perfect however. Originally the US had children saluting the flag with a Nazi salute. Somehow it feels more like the 3rd Reich after Operation Paperclip. America admired the Nazi party for its quest for global domination and became a clever copycat taking nations one by one but instead of brazenly, under the guise of fighting terrorism. This leads to the conclusion that there will eventually be an opposing force just as there was in World War II. How can we keep this force from destroying our homeland? A better question is how can we take the real America back and teach nations they face opposition when going rouge nation building. One can hardly even call it nation building when a nation is broken with no intention of being fixed. This destabilization isn't even in the interests of the US. It's as plain as day. The most powerful nation in the World is being used as a bully for external agendas with an unwitting, unquestioning public as pawns and cannon fodder. It is by design. The public are given the same Fluoride used once to keep POWs lethargic and complacent in Germany. We have become comfortably numb. Now even football the great national distraction that has kept grown men complacent for decades is failing even after millions to promote blind patriotism. Colin Kaepernick and his message about police brutality have divided the nation for a reason. These cops show signs they are being trained to be more like psycho Israeli militants who bully women and beat them down with the butt of their machine gun. Countless videos we've seen of people being beaten and shot by a police force that is supposed to "serve and protect." With all the controversy one would think that people in the Black Lives Matter movement would see the bigger picture. This is not a black and white issue as much as it is a basic rights issue. If black people understood that the US was alienating our basic unalienable right to life when the police shoots a man we would be on better footing. Anything will be done to keep this issue about race instead of basic rights. Certainly black people have the most to gain from understanding. America hides its worst side of history. The Devil's punch bowl for instance was never taught about in school because the country likes to shine as a beacon for ethics and justice instead. It loves to harvest the topic of ethics instead for power and money. Government loves the power over life and death. A power Jefferson must of known it was never supposed to have. This is what gets government high. But this is where America went astray from its foundation and became more like all oppressive governments thorough history. Do we overlook that Jefferson himself had slaves? No we do not. It is hypocritical to speak of equality on parchment saying all the right words with actions that defy them. Slavery once again reared its ugly head after all these years in the form of incarceration. The black man is still oppressed simply from another vantage. Certainly there is bias in the prison system by their numbers. Prison however again is merely government sanctioned torture. The US was never supposed to torture its citizens. Life, Liberty and the pursuit of happiness are real things. Would you be happy in a cage isolated from having any effect on the World? What about in media? Are we not all in a sort of prison in regards to bias American journalism? Who will tell the people the War on Terror is a fraud? When is someone going to have an opportunity to get on TV and lay it all out why it's not the same country anymore? You can see how priorities are misplaced when driving through Chicago. There are nearly a dozen tolls that are built like a modern fortress and between them the road is filled with giant potholes. This is perhaps the future police state. One has to eventually question the number of shootings in Chicago and how it might be related. On video a man tells his story about how crates filled with automatic weapons are simply dropped in the worst parts of town. It is as if to encourage the poorest parts of the city to have a gun fight. America loves co-opting death. We have countless movies that glorify gunfire. What would you expect from a nation that is the World's biggest arms dealer? There is said to be a black site in Chicago similar to Guantanamo bay. How is torture suddenly tolerable after Dick Cheney says it is? This isn't a country that should even allow torture. Dehumanization rears its ugly head when people like Cheney take office. The World gasped as the Deep Water Horizon spilled oil into the gulf. Benzene was poured on the water to make dead animals sink to hide them. Even hiding our mistakes that we have let loose oil on the wildlife we go further to poison our fishermen who have a livelihood that depends on it. This move that money and power come before life and all its creatures. What is the actual message of the Deep Water Horizon when Halliburton sets up bombs on the oil rig a week in advance? Is this about who is really boss in the World of oil tycoons at the expense of our wildlife? When Cascadians protest Shell we see an oil spill just south as if to say what will happen when you protest it. When Spokane wants to fine oil trains passing through town we see random oil drums suddenly leaking all over town and an oil train derailed nearly into the Columbia river. This happened just after I talked about the prospect of an oil train in the river mind you. Yes it could happen seems to be the message. Oil has become more important than the people themselves. It is called the petro dollar for a reason. If you trade in oil and dollars perhaps your nation gets a free ride. Oil feeds the war machine. Americans must come to terms that the US has a darker side. It was the side that bombed the levee during Hurricane Katrina in New Orleans. Guess who picked up the rebuilding contracts? Halliburton who Cheney was once the CEO of got to rebuild. Perhaps Kanye West was right that Bush administration didn't really care about black people. Weather weapons like hurricanes can only be used technically on your own country under international rules. You can see a vector open up where the government can simply blame the weather and rebuild a location to profit whoever they desire. Telsa invented an earthquake machine famously that shook the entire building and all of that information was gobbled up when he died by someone. At first weather modification was supposed to be for the good of all bringing rain to the desert. This was bought up to find oil and then came the government seeing an opportunity to use the weather as a weapon to an unwitting public. Strange pie shaped rainbows appear in the sky over places like China prior to a manmade earthquake and the frogs gather in the street before the ground begins to shake. Would the Chinese even know they are under attack from a foreign body? The ambiguity of weapons increases in the modern era to leave no finger prints. When we see strange rainbows in Cascadia in the news they will tell us it is from ice crystals. There is always a one liner and a pill for the public to gladly swallow. Starting a new nation built upon what is right and wrong doesn't bode well for America's interests. Exposing the true nature of the country's dark side leads people to discover racism built into the last verse of its anthem. I myself I feel have had my drink poisoned at my favorite place to eat. I nearly died shitting bloody stool. My neighbor's house was burned down to intimidate me and not a peep would be told about it in the news. When I 1st left the union in the west we have seen random acts of arson blanket Cascadia and all its territory. The Olympic rainforest caught fire for the 1st time in history and to the average person this is all coincidence due to climate change.

The Stave Vs the Bioregion

When 1st hearing about Cascadia you will likely hear about it as a Bioregion. This stance makes more sense to people who feel that an outright conflict that would likely occur with the most powerful nation in the World otherwise. People are opting instead to call it a Bioregion focusing on our regional connection to the Cascadian water shed. Protecting our water, trees and land are at the forefront of the movement on both sides. We pride ourselves on being environmentalists. Our flag symbolizes a pristine vision for our environment. Cascadia and its chapters are about establishing a regional bond that can replace allot of our need for government. It is viewed by some as a solution to the World that may ensue after a hypothetical collapse of the US. If you have seen the TV show The Walking dead you get a glimpse into a World that may happen after a total collapse of the government where normal people ironically end up being more dangerous than the flesh eating dead. The US it's self encourages that type of preparation and literally asked the public to try and be prepared for a Zombie apocalypse type event. Alexander Baretich who designed the Doug flag in 1995 calls the secessionist movement "bullshit." This likely stems from the fact that a group of people identifying as White Nationalists have created a website called TrueCascadia where they promote it. Perhaps it was created by the former government it's self as a feeble attempt to derail the movement. Who wants to be part of an equality movement co-opted by White nationalists? Certainly the people in Cascadia now are disheartened by this type of thing. For me I expect it. It tells me that I am on the right track. If you look at the hate map of America you will see all that racism and all that hate is on the east side of the country. I made a meme joking that America was burning Cascadia with its Tiki Torches. It isn't far from the truth. If anything the peace makers and the people who aren't racist are under the most attack. We can all recall how Jon Lennon who talked about long hair, peace and just staying in bed as a protest was shot in cold blood. It is as if his death and others are to put fear into the hearts of any man who genuinely desires peace and prosperity. Perhaps they are

eradicated because talking about peace embarrasses America.
I've been rapping with black people since the 90's so writing me
off as a racist is difficult for America. I suspect a portion of the
racist graffiti is done as an derailing type of attack. You would
want to make Cascadia appear more as the South did when it
tried to break away so to easily galvanize Americans who will
fight against it. The truth is I personally have already left the
union and America identifies that regardless if my fellow
Cascadians do. We are dealing with real attacks that are
ambiguous. Thousands of gallons of radioactive water have
since spilled into the Columbia river. During the Obama
Administration they joked about making Hanford a national
park to troll me. Certainly making it a national park would invite
the idea of making it a giant dirty bomb. Thousands of gallons of
sewer have been dumped into the Willamette. Is waving a
Doug flag and calling it a Bioregion going to stop these types of
attacks? Cascadians themselves in the movement are suffering
from the same cognitive dissonance. They are naive and see my
presidency as an attempt to hijack their hipster vision for
Cascadia. Talking about all this is some sort of attempt to
galvanize my presidency as some sort of self-idolatry. Much like
how Trump likely cares more about being president than taking
care of the people and the nation I am overlooked as an
outsider attempting to steal the show. Something the hipsters
have certainly worked hard to promote. It must be devastating
to see Cascadia move on without them and become an actual
government. People despise government with good reason. As
anyone can see… Calling it a bioregion under US authority does
nothing to protect the land we desire to protect. The Native
Americans are more familiar with the oppression of the US. To
this day people are being hired to slaughter the bison they
depended on for survival. This is the dark side of America they

fail to see. There is a dark side of the force. You can see it when on the news they act confused about poachers slaughtering our Elk and bears. The government likes to shoot Wolves on the news. It is meant to be intimidating. My son's middle name is Wolf. Perhaps it's unrelated. I at least consider if it intended as a message for me personally. Every other Cascadian America knows is a coward. They will set loose a fire hydrant in front of my house so I will pay attention to the water the same day Airway heights has its water contaminated. As if to ask… "How much is starting a new country worth to you?" Would it still be worth it if the west coast became a nuclear wasteland by North Korea? So long as we identify as America in the west we are in danger from the history of the US being boss on the World stage. From inside and outside the nation we could be under attack. It is smarter for me to have no national ARMY for blindsided Americans to kill? It should be a lot more like trying to track down Bigfoot. After all humans are the 2nd biggest killer next to the mosquito. Why interact? Blind patriotism creates an unthinking robot of a man willing to kill without question. It is our responsibility to make them question the country it has become. With zero state policy we are unable to remove serious modern environmental hazards like Glyphosate. With zero state policy there will remain a neurotoxin in the municipal water. Hydrofluorosilicic acid is a chemical that can eat holes through titanium and concrete. Only in an Idiocracy would it be allowed in our drinking water. Idiots can no longer be allowed to run the show. That is the final conclusion. Many people in government with a little bribery will sell their own children down the river. This is the reason there is only one legitimate government official on the entire west coast right now. Governor Brown in California neglected a gas leak in LA because his family had ties to the gas company. This is not looking out for public safety. There is a problem when money and corporations are in bed with the government. Our public health and safety pay a steep price. When people in powerful places like Donald Rumsfeld push an Aspartame agenda it is time for a limited nation state. I have a hard time seeing it in every pack of chewing gum for little kids to chew on. When you learn about the dark side of America you grow a conscience. When you are intelligent all that knowledge is useless unless you can use it to protect the ignorant. Extraterrestrials protect the ignorant when they shoot down our ballistic missiles. If you deny this is happening go and watch them talk about it on Larry King. Star visitors are protecting us from ourselves and I gave them permission May 2004. Talking about things like this perhaps makes the average person tune out. Certainly you wouldn't want to endorse a president who is talking about aliens if you don't believe in them yet. I cannot expect to have any support as president. The Noocracy may not be discovered while they are alive! It is too hard for the sheep to imagine there could be a new president without them electing one. They feel entitled to have an influence and anyone they didn't vote for doesn't deserve to be there to them. When Mrs. Powel of Philadelphia asked Benjamin Franklin, "Well, Doctor, what have we got, a republic or a monarchy?" Franklin responded, "A republic, if you can keep it." What do you think he means when he says "if you can keep it?" How can we expect to have a Republic if the majority fails to understand basic rights? Franklin was concerned about corruption in government creating a need for new masters. He said; "Only a virtuous people are capable of freedom. As nations become more corrupt and vicious, they have more need of masters. " We cannot be passive about human ignorance in the face of danger. If we understand that something is wrong with the government or its people's understanding the right to life we must cry it from the rooftops. You must say that you are mad as hell and you aren't going to take it anymore! Basic rights must be upheld by the government! There is no other basis I could of left the United States without a fire storm of bloodshed. Only with this understanding may we seek to institute new Government. Let us pause to remember how the institution of slavery goes against the declaration of independence and its vision of equality. When people finally live that sense of equality it is too late to go back. Cannons filled with silverware and nails blew through the bodies of real people over this. Racism still exists in the east. It was in South Carolina when I met with random people from the internet. We smoked a bowl on the porch and suddenly I realized they are still racist and they fought a war over this. I quickly became an outsider if I didn't delight in racist jokes. When it comes to the topic I take the approach of Morgan Freeman talking about Black history month on 60 minutes. He indicates that even if racism is still real today that the best way to handle it is to no longer give it any lime light. Story after story in the news we have seen it perhaps to purposefully divide the country or keep us distracted from topics that matter. Black Lives Matter period. There is never again going to be any fine print or sneaky wording that will strip them of their dignity as human beings. There is a powerful force I feel at play who could care less invoking cunning methods of mass sterilization of the African race. The Bill and Malinda Gates foundation for example has recently been kicked out of India for malpractice on unwitting teenagers. Perhaps feel they are being something akin to responsible stewards for the planet when it comes to the topic of overpopulation talking about it openly. You wonder if it is about race or poverty. The nature of food is exponential. If there was a World food crisis we could solve it with peas and sweet potatoes. Vaccination is the favorite vector for sneaky experimental bio-weapons. If the public is acclimated to accepting their flu shot there are new ideas such as altering the brain of those who may otherwise be violent extremists. Games can be played if the public is unwitting and trusting in their government. Trust in government goes back a long way to the 1960's in a typical station broadcast sign off in the Star Spangled Banner. Such subliminal messages like;

"Trust the US government"

"God is real god is watching"

"Believe in government god"

"Rebellion is not tolerated"

"Obey Consume Obey Consume"

"Buy ULTRA Buy"

"Worship consume believe Obey"

It reminds you of the movie They Live where Roddy Piper puts on a pair of glasses that allow him to see similar messages on Billboards and magazines all around him. In the movie he wrestles Keith David to get him to put the glasses on so someone else can see too but he refuses. They scuffle and hit one another harder and harder all over a pair of sunglasses. To Keith David Piper seems like an irrational lunatic. This is how the average person will see the Worlds smartest person if they volunteer to be the Noocracy. Einstein was seen as crazy at first and wrestled with the World so it would understand the theory of relativity. I wrestle the World much the same way about understanding our unalienable rights.

There are substantial reasons why we might not trust the US government when ARMY scientists reveal they sprayed St. Louis with a radioactive mix of cadmium for years to test radioactivity on the battlefield. Why are entire cities being used as guinea pigs? Certainly St. Louis should not be sprayed from a rooftop if you care about public health and safety.

The product "Nailed" banned in the European union for being a known neurotoxin was recently sprayed over Texas just after hurricane Harvey in a premeditated move considering there were no mosquitoes. We have to consider that like Katrina hurricane Harvey may be a weather experiment in conjunction with other agendas.

The United States government had intentionally doused 293 populated areas of San Francisco in 1950 with an unknown bacteria perhaps that is when it first began. Three days after the 49ers made their NFL debut, the U.S. Army was deployed to San Francisco and began secretly showering the city with bacteria. Over a course of eight days, a ship puttered along the shoreline of the bay, releasing massive clouds of two different pathogens *Bacillus globigii*, and *Serratia marcescens.*

A Committee on Biological Warfare was established in 1948 and part of the idea was that tests needed to be done to see if such bio-weapons would be substantial enough to use on the battlefield. The unwitting public would fall ill unsuspectedly time and time again. Such illness would be monitored. This is type of paranoia and dehumanized influence that could of only of come from attempting to match the wit and psycho numbness trying to rival German scientists of the war. It reaches the heart of dehumanization by turning a blind eye for study. There is a reason we do studies on rats instead of men. When studies are done on men revolutions happen. To match the callous will of the Germans to dominate is what invited such things as Operation Paperclip.

In 1955, as an "experiment," the CIA sprayed whooping cough bacteria over Tampa Bay, Florida. Whooping cough cases in the area subsequently increased.

In an infamous 1966 test, federal agents crushed light bulbs containing trillions of bacteria on the New York Subway, exposing thousands of rush hour commuters; the government never followed up to see how many people fell ill.

In the USA, an offensive biological warfare program was started in 1942 under the direction of a civilian agency the War Reserve Service. Initially, organisms of interest were *B. anthracis* and *Brucella suis*. Although about 5000 bombs filled with *B. anthracis* spores were produced at Camp Detrick.

When the US failed to ratify the Geneva protocol of 1925 it admitted collaboration with a suspicious group the Unit 731 scientists and was accused of using biological weapons on the North Koreans by China and the Soviet union.

As a Cascadian we feel endangered by the amount of Sarin gas being enough to wipe out all of Europe being located within our pristine region. Certainly security is still going to remain an issue even with complicit help handing us over our new government. These are the birth pains of our new nation. To overcome the darkness of our past we must humbly ask

America for its helping hand securing our future.

Being responsible about chemical and biological weapons is an international issue that should be secured with a World ARMY.

Why a Noocracy

To understand why a Noocracy one must 1st watch the movie Idiocracy Mike Judge. The movie talks about a man sent into the future in an ARMY experiment who with his average intelligence was able to save the World from its own stupidity. Many say the movie should not have so quickly became a documentary about our current state as the average person. Joe has to convince the public that water should be used on the crops instead of Brawndo the Thirst Mutilator. But you see the people suffer from the cognitive dissonance I spoke of. They believe that the plants have electrolytes and that is what plants crave! Being perhaps poor PH or too salty the drink is killing the plants and people cannot understand due to a little indoctrination from propaganda. A one liner has made the people believe that a poison that kills the plant is good for it. As the modern day Joe of our reality I see people getting poisoned with chemotherapy expecting to get well. Statistically cancer will end up with between a third and a half of the people we know. Why did America kick Harry Hoxsey to Mexico for helping too many people? I believe there is a cancer conspiracy in the US. Why else would sugar be in everything we eat? Sugar feeds cancer. Cancer is big business! This is what happens when big business gets between the people and their health. No one will see it coming. The rabbit hole goes deeper when you look at Dr. Maurice Hilliman talk about hidden cancer viruses in polio vaccines. He works at Merck the manufacturer of the SV40

Vaccine and he is giving a confession about hidden undetectable cancer viruses from Rhesus monkeys being in close proximity in your vaccines. "Yellow fever, Leukemia" are activated later in life by exposure to Formaldehyde. What is interesting is Formaldehyde pops up in a myriad of products from toilet paper, tampons to whiskey. Propyline Glycol the base for commonly used E-liquid when it deteriorates it translates into Formaldehyde. It makes you think of the original Batman movie with Michael Keaton where Jack Nicholson talks about Joker products on the news as the news anchors who use such common household products drop like flies on air as the Joker.

I found it interesting that FEMA emergency housing was loaded with Formaldehyde giving people bloody noses during Hurricane Katrina.

If there is a cancer conspiracy the Noocracy will be there to tell you about it. They will tell you that people are dumb for running with pink bows to raise money for Cancer instead of actually researching it themselves. When you are at the checkout stand they say a portion of that cancer research money simply goes to the department of defense.

At what point do people matter?

Cancer is not new however it has certainly increased after the industrial revolution. We should be asking why. In light of this I have made a special list of herbs to help people fight cancer.

In a Noocracy Taxation is theft.

Income tax… every kind of tax. When you go to buy a used car and they want a third what the car is worth. Sales tax, gas tax a tax for dying and a tax for living. The toll roads were never supposed to go up on I-405 for example. Why are people not resisting the illegal toll roads? Why have people become so complacent to allow toll roads that are charging people who don't even drive through them? Why would they allow these super police state check points to impede traffic flow? The former government is seeing how much they can get away with. They are seeing how people will bend over before there is another Boston tea party. As it turns out they will bend over quite far. They have become soft and don't care about anything unless it makes them look bad on social media. From a distance we are outraged about the animals are getting shot for sport from our keyboards. We will make a meme to save the animals in a digital universe that has no influence on reality. Everything for our generation is on a computer screen. This is because we were brought up in a World where we don't feel we have influence over reality. We feel we don't have influence over our government or our schools. We have become detached and live in a virtual World that we can control. I once tried to talk about how John Kerry was talking just like George W Bush when it came to this fraud war on terror in the paper. What good came of it? I got shot at by someone and the bullet hit the tree next to me while I was talking to a World War II veteran. Why expose what a fraud the War on Terror is when you just get shot at? Real Americans wouldn't be standing for it. Real Americans would not be occupying Afghanistan to help secure its bumper crop of Heroin when they are making safe injection sites back home as people die from it getting cut with elephant tranquilizers back home. There is a meme that says "No flag is large enough to cover the shame of killing innocent people." I think that is the real message from veterans. I think the suicide count is the real message from the troops. They would rather die than serve the US military as it is right now. When John McCain backs Al Qaeda they become confused. People don't like him probably so much that they rammed a ship named after him. The troops don't like being used. They want to have honor and stand for something good. They don't getting shot at over a fraud war just like me. Americans are confused about 9-11. They never imagined that their own government could be complicit with Israel in such a massive false flag attack. If there is no Noocracy who will tell you Netanyahu was involved? Student artists from Israel set the bombs renting a floor out of the World Trade Center.   The controlled demolition is common knowledge internationally but still denied by people on US soil. The gulf of Tonkin was another fake attack to get us into Vietnam. Saddam Hussein had no weapons of mass destruction. It was an undeclared war so why are we fighting it over a decade later? Were the sound bites about it on the news that good? The US likes to instigate War... As George Carlin said; "Because we're good at it!" I found it obliterating that Barack Obama could continue the same War on Terror Bush started. That would mean they are all the same president. We have had the same president perhaps since George Bush Sr. stood on the side of the Road watching JFK get shot. JFK warned of Secret societies. Eisenhower warned of potential misuse of the military industrial complex. Well we got both not long after. We now wonder ever since at the ambiguity of a president's power. Isn't congress supposed to stop a president from an illegal war? Congress has had a very poor rating with the people. There is a problem with the government. Its leadership can be inhibited by the bureaucracy during a time when quick change is needed. For example phosphates from fertilizer and sewage create toxic algae and the only way to stop it is to tell people to stop fertilizing their lawn. At what point should a government chose

the safety of the people over their own liberty? If you don't tell
people to stop fertilizing their lawns perhaps the lake will
become dangerous to all mammals. Does the government take
action to secure the environment? In Cascadia yes it does
because letting people just do what they want could
contaminate the only environment we have for generations.
We have a law against murder and we have laws to protect the
environment. If you believe in liberty but want to prevent your
nation from becoming some spot of land beneath the great
garbage avalanche of 2505 this is the type of government you
will have. Simple... The people must learn to take care of their
own problems. It is about teaching the people to be responsible
and adaptive for our own survival. Will the roads fill with pot
holes? Yes they will. Perhaps we should let them after 100
years of flight. We can use a website to fund anything we
desire. That is the difference. Let the people make a living wage
if they desire to fund it. It is the middle way. When the rich pool
assets it stagnates the economy. When the poor buy things it
stimulates the economy. A living wage lowers crime because
most crime is due to desperation. The rich will get mugged less
when the poor are finally provided for. It comes full circle to
benefit both ends. Why not fund the Cascadian financial
system? Many will cry that the rich will not pay their share and
that they are greedy. When you force them to pay that is not
what liberty is all about. If you believe in liberty they may opt
out of the entire financial system and refuse to donate. I believe
when you become that rich you want to give back. Life is short
and even the most greedy of the mega rich become
philanthropists. We create a vector for that wealth to give it
right back to the poor so the government can keep from
printing new money. It is ok if the government is poor. Let the
people decide if they have it at all. Every government program

can be funded individually. I would rather be a poor government financially that be on the wrong side of history. History has shown the government will tax its people into poverty. The Noocracy understands the best financial system gives its top 4th to its bottom 4th but let the people decide how much they give.

The way the US deals with homeless shows its true nature. These are people who may have full time jobs but cannot afford the rent that has gone through the roof in the dog eat dog world of landlords in a big city. At least in Vancouver BC I feel Gregor Robertson cares about the homeless by forcing people with empty houses to pay a tax. In Seattle and Spokane and Portland we see the former government sweep the problem under the rug by literally sweeping the camps themselves as if these people do not exist. That's what it says. It says they are an eye soar to the rich. To me I was disgusted when Spokane decided to replace the homeless with rocks. We do not meet the most vulnerable in our society with a bed of rocks or a bed of spikes. How dare you pretend to be my government and represent the Noocracy? We must institute a new government that cares for our safety and our happiness. When the city can afford plans for a police bunker but neglects its homeless that says that this multitude of laws to entrap the average person is more important than giving people shelter from the cold. That is what it says about us. 610,042 with more every day are homeless in the midst of empty mega churches who teach about helping them. 120,000 homeless are veterans. They will take a bullet for America then come home and live on the streets. A person on the street in LA costs 5 times as much as one if you just gave them housing. That brings us to the people who will do stupid things just to get arrested so they can have something to eat in jail. I tried to raise 20 million for the homeless. Not a dime. Pete Carroll the coach of the Seahawks put 20 million on the homeless because Seattle is his town. That is the kind of glimmer of hope we need here. That is the spirit we are trying to convey with Cascadia. Even if America doesn't do it we can. We identify with and care about the west coast more than I think America cares for us or will ever care for us. If I head east I miss our mountains. I miss it when it becomes a flat world with flat Earth thinking. Galileo probably felt the same way about the Earth being round when the Catholic Church made it flat. I have to believe that the Catholics has changed with time and now believes it is round. Even grand Churches make mistakes. All religion is a natural phase in our human evolution where we make things up to feel a closer connection to the universe. If there is a true religion it should be understanding the scientific process to find out what the truth about the universe really is. If there is a god we owe it to ourselves to find out through relentless research. Hawking says "Consideration of black holes suggests, not only that god plays dice, but that he sometimes confuses us by throwing them where they can't be seen." If we are to understand the nature of black holes we will not find our answers in religion. It is our responsibility to find out for ourselves without someone telling us an opinion. It is my responsibility in government to create a World ARMY in the wake of Albert Einstein. For all that is good in humanity we must have a tolerant World general who does not bow to the face of nationalism. We must unite to end national military rivalry. We must unite to safely end the nuclear era. I haven't told you yet. We could of stopped Fukushima from destroying the ocean. If only the people of Earth listened to the Noocracy about my warning from extraterrestrials May 2004. By design socially from things like Project Blue Book to call anyone who talks about UFOs crazy.

We have been socially engineered to call the one person who can save us from ourselves a kook. Governments love to have power and they love to have the bomb just as that monkey holding the machine gun in triumph. The bomb is a weapon that demands that our intellect be accelerated for our own survival. If it were to be misused by people who do not deserve it that could never make it in the 1st place we may be destroyed. Our confidence in missile defense is too high. It requires international control of space and all its weapons.

Already we have seen the use of beam weapons to start fires.

Arson attack is easy to start and difficult to combat once the flames get started. Directed energy weapons have now been seen as the Madeira wildfire in Portugal. Once can see that the vehicles and the road was literally melted by a weapon causing the wildfires.

We've seen directed energy weapons not only used for arson but to make atomic like explosions in Iraq.

The recent wildfire in northern California may be the same.

Don't forget northern California was always considered part of Cascadia with the State of Jefferson.

Samuel Adam's said "It does not require a majority to prevail, but rather an irate, tireless minority keen on setting brushfires in people's minds."

It makes me think of the brushfires around Wenatchee. We just passed through and they were literally burning brush to set a fire line. I would like to set a fire line myself when I see Cascadian fruit shippers burning. I really do feel our apples are under attack for being too Cascadian. Philippi fruit warehouse at 1921 Fifth Street also catches fire this year also in Wenatchee. Chelan Fruit Cooperative, lost one of its two main plants and the other was damaged in fires that destroyed other businesses and 50 to 75 residences at Lake Chelan. Underwood Fruit was on fire October 18th near Hood river.

We are talking about the possibility of paid teenage arson with smoke bombs or at least that is the cover story…

I argue that mankind learned how to make fire but doesn't know how to put the flames out. I would always tag Obama and Justin Trudeau asking for help building the World's largest firefighting fleet to avail. Communication with government officials is similar to trying to communicate with any celebrity figure. They don't communicate back. They are just images in the sky of people spammed to us that are intangible. I always wanted to be a president that finally communicates with the people. I don't mean shaking hands for photo ops and baby kissing I am talking about possibly decades or centuries of a failure to communicate.

We have all the money in the World to build machines that wage destruction… we have billions and trillions to create death but how much do we really have to save the forest?

I would take those 20 or 30 C-5 aircraft that the military has just sitting around and I would adapt them for firefighting.

I would create a grid of drones that never touch one another each pulling a little more water from the river. We deserve to bring back airships like the Hindenburg but make them safe for firefighting. I would make an H-47 Chinook with double rotors light as a feather with helium. Heavy lifting helicopters and turbine airships are the future of firefighting. Certainly the

military should also value heavy lifting aircraft. We innovate
with Co2 bombs to suffocate the fires. We create spray hoses
up the mountain with boats and jet skis in the river. We bring
back smoke jumpers. There is this idea that we should just let
the fires burn. Well I say that leads to desertification. We
should manage the forest better when it comes to overcrowded
and dead trees. When I see clear cut landscape from a plane I
think we have made a grave mistake. It's ugly what we do. You
thin the dead trees you don't clear cut my forest. We don't
need the trees gone like the forest is some commodity. To
compensate for paper we should grow hemp in Washington.
When Jeff Sessions says good people don't smoke pot I think of
George Washington who said; "Make the most of the Indian
hemp weed sow it everywhere!" I want to tell him about Carl
Sagan who made the golden record to represent mankind in
space on Voyager. I want him to Watch Sanjay Gupta talking
about how it is helping children with seizures. I want to tell him
that they used to print people harvesting hemp on the $10 bill. I
want him to watch Run from the Cure about the Rick Simpson
story in Canada. I want America to understand the extradition
of Marc Emery was a mistake because it comes down to our
failure to regulate our own mail system. It comes from our
failure to understand Cannabis after decades of propaganda.
William Randolph Hearst with the nation's largest newspaper
was worried about losing economically owning stock in timber.
Reefer madness got the best of our grandparents.
Indoctrinated since the 1930's they were taught that black jazz
musicians smoking pot were going to make babies with all our
daughters. They made it racial and they made it bat shit. You
were going to go mad and murder the town. You were going to
jump in a car... Studies show now that people who smoke
weed perhaps drive better than people who don't.

Studies were done on monkeys where they died from smoke inhalation and blamed the cannabis. Certainly if you breath any type of smoke with no air for too long your fate may be similar. They desperately want to make a story of an 11 year old who dies of marijuana poisoning so they can put all those pot heads and pot head presidents back in the slammer. The most offenses they had were those damn stoners. They need to put them in jail to keep the new private prisons at maximum capacity. America has become a prison for profit industry. Land of the free with also the most people incarcerated. The people will never add it up. They are built on being happy about the fact that other people are getting tortured. It's a big club where we are all glad we are the ones who aren't behind bars.

Government sanctioned torture is like a pig with lipstick when they try to give a person an education while they are in prison. I would like to educate that them that the government doesn't have a right to put people in a cage in the 1st place.

What laws really need to exist?

I lost a friendship with my brother in law trying to explain that there shouldn't be a law against rape. When you say something like that you get an immediate reaction. Yes rape is wrong but having a law against it means that you are going to the government for protection. To all women I say this. The government cannot protect you from rape by punishing a man as bad as a killer for choosing you as his mate. Only with good self-defense or someone to protect you can you prevent a rape from happening. By creating a law against rape you create a false sense of security that the government is going to somehow magically appear to intervene. It removes the original incentive for men to protect women. What other laws should we get rid of? Get rid of all of them and start with one law. If we are going to finally uphold our unalienable right to life there must be a law against murder. There must be a law against abortion to protect the unborn from death. Will the pink hats be upset? Yes they want to tell you about how it's ok to murder because it's murdering someone who is inside of their body. Their own blood no less. How can I raise a child of my own in this foolishness?

I would like to remind pro-choice people that we are human beings not Gerbils and we don't eat our young or sell their body parts on the black market.

What sets us apart from animals?

Women want equal rights yet does the man get to say if the child lives or dies? The man gets no choice if his own offspring lives or dies in American society if the Supreme Court fails to understand basic rights.

With a multitude of leadership beyond one person a government cannot make split decisions to protect its self.

If a meteor was used as a weapon as with the destruction of Atlantis how can the government take action if it has to get approval from a congress who can't agree on who was responsible for the attack? The Noocracy finds out who and quickly communicates about why. You do not just simply retaliate. You do not just sit around wondering who was responsible. The Noocracy will ask people questions till they get to the bottom of it.

If there is no World ARMY and no World general when there is a nuclear weapon detonated it will be mysterious who was responsible. Immediately nations retaliate without understanding who was entirely responsible. Nations may be framed with nukes. A nuke could go off in China to make it look like it was the US so that China will attack the US. Quickly without help from a 3rd party like extraterrestrials or the general of the World ARMY we lose control and Mutally Assured Destruction ensues.   A scenario like this is not far off and it is due to our negligence to form such an ARMY. Only with one source of command can the World be safe from such mystery when it comes to nuclear exchange. Only with one source of command can we by process of elimination eliminate the question of who is who in potential nuclear exchange.

Why would extraterrestrials take me more seriously than presidents and generals might you ask? They all desire power instead of mutual prosperity and stability. Corporations outgrow their desire for governments that tax them to death. Corporations also do not desire war because that is bad for international trade. Corporations if the realize it or not desire the stability such a World ARMY provides.

How can we in Cascadia isolate ourselves when we face off with international ecological terrorists? We cannot simply be passive to that type of monster. Cascadia starts as the first true international neutral zone. Foreign investors invest here because they know we are going to be leaders in the true civilization of mankind. Architects however miss the mark when they intend to give Portland a skyscraper.

Skyscrapers are irrational. They are cold hard and made of glass and metal. They are so tall that building contractors fall and die just building them and become a vector for suicide. Remote jets are flown into them and putting people in a condensed area creates a problem with pollution. People should be more spread out. A city does not represent Cascadian values but we can take steps to make them more Cascadian by making them car free in the middle.

Car culture has literally become the destroyer of life on our planet. Car culture brings things like the burning tar sands in Alberta. Half of you will be in a serious auto accident and half of the average income goes into paying for the car.

Going Cascadian is about parting from the things that have made us unhuman with one another. There is nothing human about these egos of road rage behind glass. I want people to walk down the street and say hi again. I want people to talk to strangers. I want every town to have a center where people can gather 24-7 to socialize without being considered loitering.

This entire culture of consumerism has made us forfeit our own cultures. People are losing their history around the World for a cheap chance to buy things in a mini mall. We are a society that has certain hours where our existence it's self is not welcome. That is not the type of World I want my son to live in.

Every town needs a Piano and a center.

We made a center for our town growing up in Wenatchee.

I was a rock singer in the Scary Spiders and all of us kids and our bands started putting Wenatchee on the map at the Franklin house. As time went on the city made plans of its own to pave over it the LINK bus depot. I remember as a town of angry kids and parents all gathered at the High school where we were given the plans as if there was no controversy. There was a rift between the town and its representatives. Soon the musical heartbeat of our town would be torn out like Indiana Jones in the Temple of Doom and it would paradise would literally be paved over with a parking lot ala Joni Mitchell. Upset and disgruntled people all lined up to give their 2 cents. It seems that the city was not going to budge on the idea no matter how upset we were. Rather than grabbing the mic in front of me I grabbed Mayor Tilly's microphone when I got a chance. I asked why we couldn't use the blue prints where they had a candy store in the dimensions where the Franklin house was. A person came up and saw a middle way where the two could go exist and it was met with silence.

In the Wenatchee World I was written off as a loose cannon for grabbing Tilly's mic rather than for what I said on it. They needed some youngster grabbing the mic from the Mayor to justify squashing the music of my generation with a bus depot.

I don't have any Mayors in Cascadia although people from the former government are still running for office. It is a superficial government in my eyes now. We allow it to exist. You cannot make a red blooded American a Cascadian overnight. It would backfire if you tried. They will remain willfully ignorant about Brawndo the thirst Mutilator destroying the crops until it affects them personally. I myself having a baby and understanding basic rights when no one since Jefferson has made me Cascadian. No one can tell me that I am not. I will remain a Cascadian for the rest of my life and so will my boy.

I don't think that saying you have experience has such a good track record when it comes to politicians. Experience taking a bribe from lobbyists? I only have experience being president of Orchard Middle School in 8th grade. We got to choose a special day… I got to choose hippy day. I won the election by staring at the camera and saying in a boring monotone voice that; "I'm gonna do all the stuff you guys want."

I suppose that still stands.

I would certainly like to do all the stuff you guys want as long as it doesn't infringe upon basic rights or make needless laws.

When starting a new country the sky isn't even the limit. I intend to have our own space agency that rivals NASA and Space X because quite frankly I have better ideas than they do sometimes as the Noocracy.

We are going to make a helium launch pad in the sky so we can launch smaller rockets and save money.

I hope to help build the 1st city in orbit and on the moon. I hope to make a video projector so we can communicate with these space beings that visit our orbit that yes we are listening and yes we are paying attention to these crop circles.

Communication with star visitors is one of the most important and exciting moments in human history. I am happy to say that I am one of the pioneers when it comes to close encounters. We are indeed being visited by a variety of beings and nearly all of them are far more advanced in many ways than we are.

We are seen as young and disorganized as a planet.

We are seen as undeserving of nuclear weapons and reckless with nuclear energy. As World general one of my main goals is to secure nuclear installations so that DU cannot be sold for munitions. One of my main goals is to keep nukes and dirty bombs off the black market. We cannot neglect the fact that some nations should not have the bomb yet. We cannot neglect that we have too many and too many reactors that we will not be able to maintain in the future. The number of nuclear meltdowns demands extraterrestrial intervention at this point. It is embarrassing to me that we cannot come together as a planet. It is embarrassing that we have such fractured deaf leadership when representing the human race. My own insignificance to my fellow man is an embarrassment to the human race. We live in a World where a painting from Leonardo Divinci will sell for 445 million and a living artist will not sell. I say it's because the living are dead inside. It is the people who are still alive who played it safe and failed to sacrifice themselves for the greater good. If I have no national ARMY it is either because I am a genius or have no one who believes in my vision for the nation state beyond the Bioregion. You wouldn't be able to find us. My soldiers are in every military Worldwide. They nearly have a mind of their own. Gangs infiltrated the military. Why can't ideas? An idea that multiple factions pitted against one another 24-7 is irrational. It is common sense. Global government is too abrasive when each nation has its own government. A World ARMY however with a simple transparent motive to combat terrorism conventional or environmental is much more doable. There isn't going to be any global taxation because I am the World general. Taxation is theft. It is a libertarian value. It is a Cascadian value. We let nations run themselves. We let communities run themselves. There will be no Plato Republic until the public understands the Noocracy is also necessary to secure these rights and to secure this liberty and secure our public safety sometimes. There will only be the Noocracy as government when the people are ignorant. They are the black sheep of society. The volunteer intellect steps forward with a type of understanding after decades or centuries of neglect or a failure in understanding.

The Idiocracy

When you are in a small town talking to a young teen about politics and under his ball cap he blurts out the phrase "Nuke em" you have just entered into the Twilight zone of The Idiocracy. It is built into the theme of a Neil Young song called "Piece of crap" where he talks about being disappointed by bringing home a new object that turns out to be a piece of worthless crap. It is built into a worthless medical establishment that values profit over health care. It happens when general practitioners become little more than pill pushers. It is these same pill pushers who are silently killing the elderly. I once worked at an assisted living facility where I called Bingo and washed old man butts with a rag. I came back two years later only to find out every one all 200 or so were dead. It's people putting their parents into an old folks home thinking they are doing the right thing only to find that in under two years they are going to be dead from a cocktail of pharmaceutical drugs. Ask Gaynor who lost his farm from a hay bale breaking his neck how many prescriptions they got him on... 21. We are drugging the elderly to death and turning a blind eye to it.

Everybody is doing it. Collectively we are doing something stupid and that is part of the Idiocracy. Fluoride in the water since 1939 is the biggest example.

George W Bush and the book Bushisms expose that it can run to the very top. Certainly nobody is perfect. Bush and Obama trying to make us believe Osama Bin Laden had ties to 9-11 when he had none is part of the Idiocracy. This scape goat for the War on Terror we keep hearing about who was once on the payroll of the CIA? In a documentary called Al Qaeda doesn't exist it shows CNN was strangely able to get an interview with Bin Laden. Actors were paid to stand around him with machine guns to make it look like he had actual support. We are to believe that this man is making videos when he looks like 5 different people. How stupid do they think we are? Well... In an Idiocracy they don't have to try very hard to impress you. We were supposed to believe that Khalid Sheikh Mohammed planned 9-11 from A-Z because that is what we were told. A man is going to admit to anything under torture to get it to stop.   One has to question the legitimacy of the entire process. Why has America stooped so low as to be photographed humiliating naked men on a leash with torture subjecting them to strange pop songs at high volume? The black hooded guy getting shocked before everyone internationally should not be how you want your country to be represented. Why are these torture sites only superficially shut down? What is the goal? Intimidation only works as long as people are intimidated.

Slaughtering the Bison of the Indians calling it the new national mammal while you are still doing it in 2017...

America does things to intimidate. People are too dumb to notice it's foundation on genocide of the natives and African slavery and that is part of the Idiocracy.

When only a Poke'mon phone app is able to get kids out of the house you may be living in an Idiocracy. When people dilute an important message about life and death into calling you a liberal snowflake that is part of the Idiocracy. When Mark Dice tries to offer people either a bar of chocolate or a bar of Silver and they take the chocolate you can see how they think with their stomach. People putting Splenda on their Diet Coke in the microwave is part of the problem. People putting baby formula in the microwave is part of the problem. Bisphenol A and Alex Jones turning the Frogs gay is part of the Idiocracy. Him not ever mentioning Cascadia on Infowars makes it look like a shill front for alternative media. The fact I cannot get the top chess players like Magnus Carlson to learn the new rules I wrote for chess is part of how everybody is a know it all in the Idiocracy. It starts with an unwillingness to learn new things. It starts when people would rather consume than feed their mind nourishment. The focus of the brain moves to the impulsive side when thinking about base instinctive things like wanting food. With the mind there is an incentive to use it or lose it. When we focus on deep memory we are able to unlock a part of the brain that has more time to think. If you keep your eyes closed when you 1st wake up for example the mind is able to more easily remember the dreams you had that night. If you open your eyes suddenly those dreams will vanish as the brain is now focusing on processing your surroundings. What you focus on will build that part of the brain and that type of thinking. In Hypnosis people are more able to remember things by moving brain waves from the wakeful Beta state quickly to Alpha if you roll your eyes back in your head. By calming you are able to take the mind into Theta and Delta brain waves slower and slower allowing more time for the brain to process data. By doing so people seem to be able to remember what they wished for on their 7th birthday or perhaps even a previous life. Regardless if you believe in reincarnation some scientific evidence speaks to life after death. A video of a mouse dying in a mouse trap pops up on the internet and one can see at the exact point of death a little ecto spirit lifts up from the mouse body. People have been shown to technically weigh slightly lighter just after death. I have seen similar white ecto spirits in other photographs. I have a unique photo of my brother was a quadriplegic at the time during Bumbershoots. I would ride around on the back of his chair like he was Timmy from South Park. In the photo you can see a similar white ecto spirit flying in front of him with the space needle and an actual UFO all in the same shot. People have recorded multiple cases of near death experiences and also recall previous lives. My stepdad From germany for instance seemed to remember a previous life when passing through Montana.

We are idiots if we don't try to understand life after death scientifically. A boy named Cameron remembers a detailed previous life on the remote Scottish island of Barra. When he arrives he recognizes it and longs for his previous mother who he misses. He was able to the say the name of his previous dad and that he died in a car accident.

James Leininger just toddler points to a picture of Iwo jima to his parents and says that "This is the place where my plane was shot down." As it turns out only one plane was shot down there in 1945 at the end of World War II American pilot James Huston Jr. He correctly stated that his ship was The U.S.S. *Natoma.*

Shanti Devi 1926 born in India said her real home was Mathura. She claimed to have died 10 days after giving birth to her child. She said the name of her husband who was found in Mathura who also claimed the same was true. This case was also researched by Mahatma Gandhi.

The Pollock Twins appear to be the reincarnation of their own dead sisters killed a year before they were born in a car crash. When the family moved away for 4 years and returned to the same town the twins were suddenly able to point out land marks they had never been to before. They remembered the school and were able to name each of their old toys when shown.

A boy named Hunter remembers being legendary golfer Bobby Jones. Also an amazing golfer at the age of 7 he is doing 41 out of 50 Jr. Tournaments.

Barbro Karlen from Sweden claims to be Anne Frank in her last life. At age 10 in Amsterdam she told her parents that they didn't need a cab because she understood exactly where she was. She took them to the house and strait to Anne Frank's hiding spot.

Edward Austrian had a spot on his throat he called his "shot." He describes being a soldier named James during World War 1 walking through the mud in France. He remembers getting shot in the back of the neck having it fill with blood after going through somebody else.

A boy at age 3 remembers a man and claims that it was his neighbor who killed him with an axe. The boy ironically has a mark where the axe wound was like many of these cases do that symbolize a previous cause of death. His face goes white and the boy proceeds to point out where he we buried where they find his skeleton. The skull with a clean axe wound.

Chanai Choomalaiwong from Thailand remembers being a teacher on his way to school and convinces his parents to visit his previous life as Bua Kai Lawnak. He was brought in after showing his birth marks and asked to him to pick out Bua Kai's belongings.

There is a phenomenon in Hypnosis called past life regression.

Beyond these findings we can now take into a peek of how this works. While moving down to our lowest brain waves with a calming verbal sedation the hypnotist attempts to have the subject visualize walking on a beach. As they walk down the beach they attempt to remember earlier and earlier times in their life and describe them. We try to get them to remember their earliest memories as a 2 year old. Suddenly there is a fog that represents the part of the mind that is blocking you from recalling your last life. The subject was slowly walking through the fog and when they come out the other side strangely have access to memories that are inaccessible with faster brain waves that were dormant.

The conclusion is that we have to consider that we either have these memories imprinted and dormant at birth in the brain or we are getting the brain to access what some might call a collective consciousness. If it the latter we have to think that the universe has a sort of hive mind where we can reach in and remember people or that those people are with us when we are born. How to determine what is happening cannot simply be accomplished with brain scans but doing them under a deep past life regression is one of the next steps.

There are books where a plethora of 50 cases or more where people describe similar things just after they die where after a dramatic death memory of perhaps getting slain with a hatchet they are met by a tunnel of light and at the end describe a feeling of infinity. They describe a feeling of timelessness.

In the case of the boy and Barra island he remembers going down a hole in Barra and suddenly being born again. In his case it implies and almost immediate return. However in Hypnosis people describe the ability to portray yourself in any shape or form you desire. Similar to how our profile pic in social media can be anything we desire but in a mental universe.

If there is a collective consciousness I feel I encountered it once while on LSD. It was the fishing trip. We went fishing with some friends and some tracers on the fishing pole. Nothing out of the ordinary of any other acid trip I had had. I was listening to Tool and the Beatles earlier in the day and suddenly I heard a Tool song clear as day but with no headphones in my ears. It didn't seem possible. I had somehow made time slip and was hearing an earlier part of the day. That was strange. I go to take a piss in the park urinal and remember this crude looking guy taking a piss next to me. He seemed so disgruntled about life and on a low vibration in an irked state of mind. I realized that it was the polar opposite of my state of mind. I was curious about nature in awe looking at its roots in the dirt. I was having fun. I walked across the bridge and suddenly all the rocks started spinning in the same direction. As the paint on the end of a prop on a plane you can see an entire circle. If there was a speck of black on a rock you could see a perfect ring all the way around it. I smoked a bowl with my friends while they were fishing and suddenly the trip seemed overwhelming. I sat down and put my head in my hands suddenly zooming out into what I believe is the Collective consciousness. I was never able to reach it before or since in my entire life. It was like melding with the mind of god. I was able to see the infinite nature of the universe. I was finally in a state of mind where I could be receptive of the infinity. This was bigger than just zooming out from my body into space as I had done before. This allowed me to see every path that I may take in my life. Imagine instant thought and only one instance where time is no longer linear. It is life being is being played on a record. Perhaps the past and the future are fixed but we must be allowed the perception of free choice. Jim Carey recently is saying things "There is no Jim Carey" from preparing to play the part of Terrance Mccenna. It is a unique state of mind. That energetically from the base that makes up all matter we are all technically the same person. As if we must become born as separate entities for god to be curious again. It is an idea that everything is god. God cannot be separate from everything or we will say that there is no god. We are all the same god. By nature god wants to find out if we have separate bodies if we will create new thoughts. I feel as the World's smartest man god must be bored like I am so life is created. Without physics and the spectrum, without matter without life and separation from the collective there can be no new thought and no new input. We are left with English to fumble to describe a dimension that is boundless. Without separation there can be no identity. God wants you to have an identity so that your ego becomes boundless. To have the ego of god you must 1st have the ego of Jim Carey.

I talk about god because Albert Einstein believed there must be a god and that science brings us closer to understanding god. My point is that talking about god does not make you an idiot because certainly he was not an idiot.

Einstein said; "I fear that technology will surpass human interaction. The World will have a generation of idiots."

A statement like that rings true today with the Pokemon' Go app. We will be lead around by a video game across town but no longer know who our neighbors are.

What makes humanity an idiot?

Since you won't take a word from me...

Einstein said; "Insanity is doing the same thing over and over again and expecting different results."

In an Idiocracy we do things the same way expecting different results. Take for instance how we respond to hurricanes. We say; "Will Rebuild" like hurricanes are some kind of joke. We don't take our own survival seriously. We are so blacked out by entertainment that we fail to migrate to a different region when presented with hurricane statistics. The people must move from hurricane alley. It is irrational to make an investment in the gulf and Atlantic coast because it will be subject to permanent future hurricanes.

We must be a civilization that adapts to climate change.

New types of wind turbines are being built to harvest hurricane force winds. That is how you adapt. Are you going to stay there? You certainly better adapt to hurricane force winds!

That starts with architecture.

If we build the same cookie cutter architecture and just say that we will rebuild whenever there is a natural disaster we are idiots. Every house block to block is built the same way as the ones we see flattened by tornadoes. Do we just sit around and droop about how sad it is we lost our houses without making any actual changes as architects?

Our architects are building for looks and for money. What we need are architects that build for blending with nature impervious to natural disasters.

Our survival is at stake and no changes are being made. I predict houses will all look the same at the end of my life time because this is an Idiocracy where people fail to listen to the Noocracy.

You build houses into a sound hill so water runs past to prevent flooding. You build with earthquake bags instead of wood. Stop chopping down my forest you idiots. Grow hemp on the Columbia basin to enrich it's soil and build with hempcrete because its several times lighter and stronger than concrete.

Build your roofs with insulated transparent polycarbonate roofing so you can grow food in extreme climate conditions. This is so important.

When I see the homeless crisis I want to teach mankind that we have been building our own homes the wrong way all this time. It is time to relook at the way we build our houses.

In spite my arguments about skyscrapers the World Trade Center wasn't built cheaply. It was designed to withstand multiple airline jets without collapsing. Each plane would have gone in like how it is when you poke a pencil through a screen door. Mankind is not completely stupid. This building could have burned for weeks and it wouldn't have come down.

Professor Steven E Jones of BYU lost his job telling you the truth about demolition on 9-11. There are people who are brave about the truth. A skyscraper Is a good building for people to climb during the next ice age as the snow becomes higher and higher.

I think that due to mass stupidity if the snow grew to 100 feet we would kill ourselves with carbon monoxide from all our cars attempting to travel and all our generators attempting to heat our houses at the bottom. The gas will slowly blanket the street level and the following symptoms follow...

- Dull headache

- Weakness
- Dizziness
- Nausea or vomiting
- Shortness of breath
- Confusion
- Blurred vision
- Loss of consciousness

Families may collapse and die Worldwide simply because we were too stupid to switch from gasoline to water and it's hydrogen.

Mass stupidity could easily make a nuclear exchange get out of hand. We don't have to wait for the Antarctica ice sheet to melt and slow the current of the ocean for the next ice age we might make one over night with a Nuclear winter in our own stupidity.

Even knowing that ice ages are cyclical through history we fail to prepare for one. Even as we dig up the Covis points that they found in my 1st grade teachers Orchard…   we fail to prepare for our own ice age.

We used to make long blades of obsidian shaved off beyond razor sharp off the knee. Making Clovis points was an art and we used them on spears to hunt the Wooly Mammoth. Sadly there are claims that we might bring the Mammoth back but no one is able to find ample soft tissue. Just yesterday on the news Trump is lifting a ban from the Obama administration that blocked the import of Elephant trophy hunting ivory. As 1st president of the Northwest I can take some action. I can import elephants to protect them. Perhaps they will adapt to the colder climate if we put them on the coast. But as World general… If I am allowed as World general to take action to protect the wildlife of planet Earth this would be final step we require to take real action to protect the life of Earth. Hunting is not a sport. Mankind will likely kill all the animals because of this type of mentality. I worry for the fish. Fukushima has tainted the fish and rivers are too warm. There are too many dams and the sea lions are cutting off the river. I fear for all the animals that survive on fish if our overfishing dooms us. Overfishing the ocean will have a big effect on many other species. Fishermen are saying they have seen the ocean go dead where it once had fish. The Kelp we use to help with radiation has it's self been vulnerable to absorbing radiation. I have posted nearly 400 stories about Fukushima on the internet.

At the end of the day it only reaffirms my quest to build the World ARMY. If there is a nuclear disaster it should be dealt with by an international body not by the same people who try to sweep the problem under the rug. Cutting edge ideas can be used to secure such nuclear disasters and an international body has to supersede and cooperate with the company responsible. As the World's smartest man even I am likely to come up with some of the best ideas how to deal with a nuclear accident. For instance we inject the core with liquid nitrogen and boron. We dump a lead mixed borax concrete on the fucker from helicopters and cranes. Before that we do a dig to bowl beneath the core. Putting radioactive water into the ocean over and over endlessly was not a good plan. This is part of the Idiocracy.

Fukushima seemed like an unnatural tsunami. I suspect foul play. Who would be so cruel to Japan? Who would be so bold and cruel to our whole planet? Did they understand what would be the outcome of their actions? I cannot assume to know.

The only one who pretends to know is Benjamin Fulford and what he says could lead one on a wild goose chase.

I believe however believe that the prospect for manmade tsunami's exist and perhaps have been tested.

These new vectors of intimidation must be identified if they exist. People like Richard Boylan will talk about a secret Cabal with super weapons. If there is such a secret Cabal it must be identified. We are near a new wave of technology that could put tools of robot assassination into the hands of any rouge idiot. New measures must be taken internationally to secure corporations from building mass production of robot soldiers.

What I am saying is this could get out of hand really fast.

If no one is at the helm on planet Earth...

If it is ambiguous who is the Captain Picard of Star ship Earth...

We are in danger having fractured leadership.

This resistance for a ship captain must be quickly done away with because for a myriad of reasons we are going to need one.

If we start a serious exchange...

Earth needs leadership.

If we encounter hostile aliens...

Earth needs leadership.

When we don't diversify and grow enough food for the people Earth needs leadership.

When we have beatings in the street and everybody just stands around watching it happen.

Earth needs leadership.

When there are intentional oil spills to piss off people saying "Water is sacred"

Earth needs leadership.

I think of Chief Seattle with its modern gentrification pushing the poor out of town...

I think about how he talked about how the white man thinks of property that he owns the land when he does not.

The natives believed that we belonged to the land instead.

The land does not belong to us.

We have this idea that we own the World. That we can buy a little piece of it but that kind of thinking doesn't allow for such things as nomadic seasonal animal migration when you have a barb wire fence everywhere you go. We are being imposing on the landscape. We build roads made of tar that locks heat because it's black. We aren't thinking about being more sensitive toward road kill. We instead just make it ok to bring them home for supper. One day there will be no animals because red necks will have shot them all for pleasure.

When it comes to bans I cannot just ban things left and right or the anarchist surface and would be upset with me. I ban things like the former government from killing our animals with hired poachers.

Who among you will identify these random arson attacks in the west? Who among you will stand up against arson in Cascadia?

Who will report the names of these poachers if they are hired to kill our animals?

What policeman will quit their job to join the Cascadian ARMY to have a job with no pay?

If I had a national ARMY it would be to stand at the I-405 toll roads with nothing bug Doug flags.

If I had a national ARMY it would be to stand at the border of Mexico as well as Canada with Dougs.

I am Cascadian all the way to Alaska!

Do you think we really want people like Sarah Palin shooting our wolves from a Helicopter like it's a video game?

These people should not be in power.

As the Noocracy I might be #1 at Star Craft and Leauge of Legends but I learned to separate video games from reality.

Do you really think we deserve to have Fallout Cascadia happen here in the northwest?

Fallout Cascadia...

The intro goes something like this:

When the United States military went rouge after 9-11
under the guise of fighting terrorism some felt it was time to part ways.
Ecological terrorism instead had taken the front seat when
Halliburton blew up the Deep Water horizon oil rig in the

Atlantic. We knew something big was going on. 1st to leave the Union was a man named Adam Brisbine who felt that the United States never upheld our unalienable rights or execution, abortion and lethal force by police would not exist. He was inspired by Jefferson from the declaration of independence because it said he had a right to leave the union. Unsatisfied with leading the World by example as an isolationist he sought to claim himself 1st general of the World ARMY to end national military rivalry and that's when things got ugly. The powers from inside and outside the continent hungry to be the dominant force set loose a fire storm upon the northwest in spite of it being claimed as an ecological sanctuary and an international neutral zone. But in the desolate Puget Sound once bubbling with nuclear fire something still moves. In the wreckage of Seattle some remember the day mankind tried to make a difference in the name of prosperity and failed horribly.

The fact that there is such a thing as…"The Children of Atom" in Fallout makes me wonder if there is such a thing as time travel or perhaps someone paying attention. I changed my name to Atom in my divorce legally in 2008. Later we see the Intel Atom Processor. We see Atom in the movie Real Steel where there is a robot with the name. It is ironic? It might be irresponsible for me to allow a new World of automated killer robots. Certainly I could train the robots to be good at martial arts if I am not careful just by posting videos. I worry of a super battalion of a Robots I do not control that can get 30 and 0 on Counter-strike like I can in the real World who can fight as good as I can or better. Robots can be designed to fire better and fight harder than any man at this point. Perhaps sex robots could be programmed to go rouge and something like that could be just around the corner. An automated future is a police state wet dream. Everywhere you go you are recognized. There is a good and bad side to this. Without the Noocracy at the helm it could easily go from the global surveillance system used to track terrorists to an oppressive unthinking machine that executes based on body language analyzes and facial expressions.

Someone seen as angry by the system may simply be taken out lethally for making the wrong face. First the government would have to understand every person has an unalienable right to live even terrorists.

There is a reason you don't simply kill terrorists.
If we are to simply go in to a building and kill our Osama Bin Laden that fails at more than protecting his right to life, that fails as protecting national or global security. You must take a terrorist alive to ask them questions about further terrorism. It is irrational for the government to tell us it is smart or ethical to simply take one out. If they do it is likely the person is simply a patsy for a hidden agenda.

Fake shootings and bombings are happening Worldwide apparently as an effort to prepare for this kind of leadership I hope. I suspect these fake bombings and shootings are done to acclimate the public as well as responders to real situations. Passing them off as real on national television is a bit over the top however and spawns animosity for the government.

The Murder of Allison Parker and Adam Ward live on WDBJ7 I believe is one of these fake shootings. One can see that the woman is not really getting shot during the video and that blanks are being used. Poor acting lack of wounds and a photo of them with fake wounds and make up smiling for the camera just prior make it pretty hard for a keen eye to swallow.

The Boston Marathon bombing was fake. They used fake smoke bomb type explosives with fake crisis actors and fake blown off legs the works. It was interesting to see a premonition of it on Family guy as well.

During the LAX shooting a man was seen pushing a dummy on national television in a wheelchair.

Actors were paid to rejoice when a statue of Saddam Hussein was pulled down in Iraq.

Mosques were blown up and blamed on Mossadeq... Then eventually the Shah of Iran was also replaced.

Bruce Edwards Ivans killed himself when he found out he was to be blamed for the Anthrax envelopes after 9-11. Later were documents found that the Anthrax was to be blamed on Al Qaeda.

Some of these are footing blame creatively. Some of these are propaganda to make it seem like the Iraq war was a good idea if not a triumph. Some of these are perhaps about gun control. Some of them are about emergency preparedness. Some perhaps are to incite a general fear in the population. Perhaps a fake event will be mixed with real bullets to give the public a feeling of overwhelming odds if they were to attempt to cast off their tyrannical government.

I can only speculate what the Vegas shooting was about. You can see the photos of the body with guns around him you have to wonder about the core message. People are scared about the Vegas shooting more than the others because real bullets were flying. It's unmistakable. It is considered the largest mass shooting next to things like Wounded Knee. One has to note after all the hub bub in the media for a few days there appears footage of a helicopter with unmistakable machine gun fire coming from it. You could consider that a huge piece of missing information from the official story. We were lead to believe it was a lone gunman. People talk of the esoteric hidden meaning of the Vegas shooting as an Illuminati blood sacrifice next to a pyramid. Perhaps it is a warning for Cascadia not to expand into Nevada. Certainly there are places the US government would like to protect in Nevada like Area 51. Strangely it was said the people were warned ahead of time they were all going to die by a Hispanic couple.

There are different definitions of Idiocracy.
Mine is:

"A government that has failed to adequately look after public health and safety for over a decade."

Idiocracy
Function: Noun
Definition: a form of government in which a country or territory is run by fools
Example Sentence: Some democracies can turn into idiocracies depending on the election results.

The description of the movie it's self is very telling.

1. Idiocracy

Idiocracy is a 2006 American satirical science fiction comedy film directed by Mike Judge and starring Luke Wilson, Maya Rudolph, Dax Shepard, and Terry Crews. The film tells the story of two ordinary people from the present who take part in a top-secret military hibernation experiment, only to awaken 500 years in the future in a dystopian society full of extremely dumb people. Advertising, commercialism, and cultural anti-intellectualism have run rampant and dysgenic pressure has resulted in a uniformly stupid society devoid of intellectual curiosity, social responsibility, and coherent notions of justice and human rights. Despite its lack of a major theatrical release, the film has achieved a cult following.

America never really gets a true democracy. The popular vote does not really count. We have seen it. Don't for get the Don't taze me bro incident where a college student was hit with a Taser asking John Kerry why he stepped out after winning the 2005 election. Al Gore beat Gorge W Bush yet the public vote did not matter. Don't call America a democracy. Your votes have not mattered for a long time. It's more of a feel good thing. You went out and you felt like you made a difference. It would be a grand experiment to let the people have a true democracy however they would 1st have to understand why I left the union from the US. You have to get the average idiot to understand basic rights and this is difficult. It proves more and more difficult and may never be accomplished in my lifetime. Someone else would have to take Jefferson literally. As with the 1st dancer phenomenon at the Gorge amphitheatre someone has to make understanding our unalienable right to life cool and hip enough to want to join in the dance! If we were to make understanding basic rights a common concept we quickly see how we are living in an occupied Cascadia. There is US occupation in the media to make it seem like America as if everything is business as usual. There is occupation in law enforcement whenever there is use of lethal force they are violating our basic unalienable rights. The police are enforcing the law of the former government by willful ignorance and by occupation.

The truth is you don't have to go to the court of the former government. You don't have to go to jury duty. You don't have to feed into that system. You don't have to pay that fine. It's called civil disobedience. You don't have to acknowledge the United States in Cascadia and when you play that same game that they play ignoring us we can take the power back. You see there doesn't have to be bloodshed. Cascadians and Americans can coexist just like people from Canada often frequent Washington. There doesn't have to be some kind of civil war. This is about being a Cascadian personally. You make the choice. I am not going to oust the former governor with the Cascadian ARMY. I don't have to. A grass roots movement starts from the bottom up not the top down. We make it so Cascadian that the governor will recognize it and finally choose to resign.

You who fail to understand basic rights you are the Idiocracy. You presidents and Supreme court justices are the Idiocracy. It is an utter colossal failure in leadership Worldwide.

You who fail to adapt to climate change are the Idiocracy. Are you prepared domestically for 200 degrees to minus 200 degrees? We should be.

Should we have special masks and more options for oxygen in the wake of a heavy volcanic explosion or forest fire?

We face the prospect of nonstop fire every summer. Do you have a HEPA filter in your house? Do you have multiple?

Do you save your seeds at the end of every season? If you don't you are part of the Idiocracy.

Can your city make fire from snow to heat themselves this winter? If it cannot your city is part of the Idiocracy. You have not adapted and your city may die of carbon monoxide in deep snow.

We must also face the prospect of adapting to drought. Drought is easy to create with super weapons. You may experience a dry year and have to adapt by making atmospheric water generators. Even low tech atmospheric gathering can be accomplished with a little ingenuity. Low tech and cheap tech ideas are the future. I invented a thermoelectric window you can install in a regular window to create silent power from the difference in temperature of outdoor and indoor air. I used to use Thermoelectric Peltier TECs to cool the Celeron 366 processor to a frosty cool with spray foam all over my mother board to get the fastest speed possible. I think I might of broke to 866 by finally attaching it to the garden hose and running that through my water block into the basement shower below! I figured if you take a window on each side you can use cheap glass and reverse the concept by instead of powering them use them to create electricity with 20 in series. Simple... ideas that have little environmental impact are the best. What does it take some ceramic and a little metal? Asking people to make HHO to heat themselves is potentially dangerous if you are an idiot.

Hydrogen is very volatile and it pops like a bomb. I had a jar on the front porch blow by using caustic Sodium Hydroxide with foil and it blew an Adam's peanut butter lid so hard the whole neighborhood could hear. You have to learn about safety pop off systems and use very small tubes and openings with consistent pressure.

People are idiots when they light up pumping gas.

They fart allot. I know for a fact.

Do you think Robbin Williams killed himself?

Do you think George Carlin died of a heart attack?

It's a good question. There has been a heart attack gun since the 70's. It makes one wonder when it is a leading cause of death.

Prince was killed on the Simpsons and the guy was saying "because certain people won't do what we want!" Homer whacked Prince...

The Simpsons strangely had symbolism predicting 9-11. Someone holds a Magazine to Bart that says NEW YORK $9 with the Twin towers in the background to make 11. And there is an Iconic representation of Donald Trump going down an escalator with a sign that drops in the same location!

You become curious. There is premonition of 9-11 in the movie Back to the Future with multiple symbolism. Also Neo's passport in the Matrix says Sept 11th 2001. They call this phenomenon Predictive Programming.

It was determined by John B Watson in his research in the 1920's that our behavior is dictated by fear and not love. It is easy to capitalize on by pumping fear stories into the media. It puts you on edge. The CIA has been involved in keeping that fear alive in the media since the 1950's.

Part of gaining independence is having an independent newspaper. An independent media must be created when starting a new country. If not your revolution will be omitted indefinitely.

What is the CIA? If it is the center of all intelligence I must beg to differ. I am the center of all intelligence. I am the center of all people.

On my IQ test it said I was a word warrior.

If I am a warrior I would like to use that for the good of all people by ending all national conflict forever.

With higher intelligence comes higher fears and higher responsibility. You protect the lives of millions then billions. You can protect people better from disasters by prevention. One could prevent oil spills with a World ARMY. One could prevent burning oil fields with a World ARMY.

One of the 1st things I want to do is stop annual marine slaughters. I will make a physical presence to save the Pilot whale on Faroe Islands.

We can let Sea Shepherd lead a fleet before it starts. I would let the World know it's here. I would let the World know I mean business. You can't have fucking annual marine slaughters because I have a culture too and it entails stopping mother fucking poachers and slaughtering internationally.

So now I would like to talk about how civilized people fight. We publically say if they want to slaughter dolphins that they will have to fight over it with bare hands. We stand in the way and go to town in a glorious hand to hand combat with ambulances on standby ever year. That is something I will fight for. That is fighting I can believe in. The troops have a moral problem because occupying a foreign country to be Israel's little bitch or to occupy Afghanistan to run a serious underground heroin operation is not what they signed up for. They don't like fighting Al Qaeda or ISIS if the US it's self is funding, directing or giving weapons to the guys they are supposed to be fighting against. Just think Blaine Cooper talking about John McCain calling him a traitor in that town hall meeting. That is how the troops feel.

The troops wanted Ron Paul to be president. If you wanted to support the troops why didn't Ron Paul become president? I will tell you why. Because the Idiocracy.

Sunshine Minting in Coeur d'Alene, Idaho was printing the Liberty dollar and they were raided in November 2007 and silver stolen. Perhaps their coins were too similar to US coins. Remind me to make the Cascadian dollar to stand out and look unique and different than US coins. But remember JFK wanted a new currency. JFK signed executive order No. 11110 to allow the US to issue its own currency without going through the Federal Reserve. JFK was killed just 5 months later. This was meant to be a warning to future presidents who attempt to tinker with the Federal Reserve.

Just the same America should not be intimidated by such darkness. The America I know would stand up and abolish the Federal Reserve from printing presidents too.

Andrew Jackson was one of the 1st to see the problem. He used his veto to say:

"It is not our own citizens only who are to receive the bounty of our government. More than eight millions of the stock of this bank are held by foreigners… is there no danger to our liberty and independence in a bank that in its nature has so little to bind it to our country? Controlling our currency, receiving our public

moneys, and holding thousands of our citizens in dependence...
would be more formidable and dangerous than a military power
of the enemy. If government would confine itself to equal
protection and, as heaven does its rains, shower its flavor alike
on the high and the low, the rich and the poor, it would be an
unqualified blessing. In the act before me there seems to be a
wide and unnecessary departure from these just principles."

Abraham Lincoln was vigilant to prevent the Rothschild's from
funding the civil war. We have to remember he also attempted
to print the Green back. Follow the money. When they found
Booth's diary from Stanton's troops they found names of co-
conspirators linking him to Judah P. Benjamin, the Civil War
campaign manager in the South for the House of Rothschild.

You will find them blatantly saying interesting cocky historic
quotes when you look deeper. It is one thing for the president to
understand the situation it is entirely different for the people to
understand as well. They must be educated!

"Who controls the issuance of money controls the government!"
–Nathan Meyer Rothschild

They are all singing the same tune!

"I care not who controls a nation's political affairs as I control her
currency." –Mayer Armschel Rothschild

The Money Masters... The Money Mafia...

What if I told you the Noocracy is more powerful than all of
them?

Power starts in the mind.
Knowledge is power.

Jefferson nearly left California to become its own state to join Oregon but the vote was the day after Pearl Harbor. December 8th 1941... That is interesting because it would have been a great distraction. Also note that America was aware the Japanese were coming to attack ahead of time. It seems America was asking to get attacked by putting so many ships in the same spot. That is going to be intimidating.

If you make yourself the most knowledgeable person that ever lived what does that mean?

There are different kinds of knowledge. There are different types of awareness. Let's review some of the World's brightest minds.

Ben Pridmore can memorize a deck of cards in 24 seconds. He does it by using symbolistic objects in his mind to recall the entire deck. For fun he memorizes the 13 digit barcode of every item in his shopping bag. The barcode for sweets is 5010317040526

He says he turns the numbers into pictures...

He says for lemons it was "A lemon being fed to a Sasquatch wearing a plastic bag concealing a pack of sausages and a leg."

A Sasquatch is the symbol of Cascadia if you think about it. A Sasquatch must be also genius for being able to hide from humans for so long. We have to also consider the intelligence of the Neanderthal having a larger brain. It seems we killed them in fear of something. Imagine if we killed them in fear of their intelligence! A single shelled skull is also superior to a sectioned skull like ours. Mistaken for an inferior species were apparently superior in some ways. We still carry about 4% of their DNA today. We obviously had a few human Neanderthal relationships. If they are related I cannot tell. I have however seen enough photographic evidence now to call myself a believer. Eventually you see enough to be convinced. I have never seen a Sasquatch but I believe!

Rumor has it giant bones of humans were destroyed at the Smithsonian. Giant men would also have larger brains. Dolphin brains are twice as large as ours. If we gave dolphins the ability to use tools underwater perhaps they would build a city in the deep blue! We have to wonder if some extraterrestrials might be more interested in them than us. We can only wonder how complex they are socially. It makes you think of Star Trek the Voyage home when they uncloaked in front of a whaling boat and the harpoon bounces off the ship to their dismay. As we have little care for whales in the ocean whales are killed to this day under the guise of being science research specimens. Sea Shepard stalks them on the open ocean. Our deep sonar may be disrupting sea life. Oh well. We must have nuclear reactors floating in the water apparently to maintain a national aura of supreme intimidation. I think we should have an awakening about treading lightly on mother Earth. How can anyone tell large countries to stop over fishing. In the end you know that people do not listen until it is too late. We make problems and deal with them when they happen on the fly collectively instead of taking preventative measures to stop them from happening in the 1st place.

Kim Peek the original inspiration for Rain man is a human encyclopedia. We ironically call a man with remarkable memory a person with Savant Syndrome and brain damaged. A man who can remember nearly any facts without parallel because he remembers 98% of what he reads with ease. Soon only artificial intelligence will be able to rival his mind. We are biological computers. Electronic computers can actually now process data faster and broader than the human mind. There is an acceleration of the A.I. mind that is not like the human mind it is exponential. Learning computers will change everything. The computer has always beat me at high levels. I am happy to say that for the 1st time ever this year I have beat the computer.

Even if A.I. surpasses the human Rain man encyclopedia a computer cannot create ideas yet. It is the creative computer I am curious about. To advertise for what I feel was the 1st real home computer the Adam computer they called it "The creative computer." A woman naked was eating an apple to insinuate Adam and Eve before tape drive box on the desk. Ironically my dad bought a Coleco Vision and a Commodore 64. We suddenly had the 1st Color computer at home and when I got to school I realized the Apple II we had playing Oregon Trail was lagging far behind what we had at home. I once went to a computer club meeting and on 5 inch floppy disks were nearly 1000 video games just sitting there waiting for the public to play them for the 1st time a new window was going to open that is a mirror for our articulate thoughts. Since 1995 we have had a very powerful multitrack recorder in Cool edit pro allowing over 100 tracks of audio. It becomes a part of your life as you layer multiple tracks of audio and multiple ideas. It compounds the ability of one person to become as many people to play the music as they desire only limited by their ability to play. The computer allows a thousand things to be done simultaneously that you control. We have gone so far from calculators that were the size of a living room to what we have today. I can see such ideas as holographic integration in the future having a profound influence over our reality. Already we have surpassed the Dick Tracey wrist watch. The progress of our advancement in computers seems exponential. However I can also see in an Idiocracy that people may one day lose their ability to create them due to a failure in automation in their manufacture. When machines and computers themselves create the computers we become lost how to make them from scratch. We face possible roll backs in technology simply because we forget how to do things. Such a rollback would be significant if we cannot understand how to build a basic computer. Understanding that all computer memory is vulnerable to the test of time is important to get use to a drive in the direction of crystal memory. Only with crystal memory may all this information truly last. In this way computers are still in their infancy. We have not yet acclimated to a memory type that lasts. Solar events and magnetism can cause our memory to fail. Mechanical hard drives that still spin may run faster in the moment but are not as viable as an option due to moving parts. If magnetic spin type generators are able to give us electricity they will eventually break due to magnets slapping together and a failure from moving parts. Even if we make them they risk wiping our fragile computer memory. The integration of computers the government will get the best of us if we allow it to create too many laws. The average person will become a victim of an automated surveillance system. If the government doesn't yet understand our unalienable right to life there could be killer robots that kill people who make certain facial expressions indicating anger when holding an object. If you've ever wondered why people hide their faces in a protest it is acknowledgement of facial recognition technology. There is a reluctance for people to want to disclose where they were and who they were with because of the idea of guilt by association.

George Washington said "It is better to be alone than in bad company."

I think that rings true today when it comes to nations.

There is a College Humor skit called 'Why America is like a bad boyfriend.' A girl breaks it to her friend that she is in a bad relationship. She denies it and says that she loves her country. "Then why is he sneaking into all your E-mails?"

"Then why is he always borrowing money when he's in debt?"

"Then why is he always getting into fights?"

She claims he is actually breaking up fights!

"He is getting in a fight right now!" and you can see him beat a man's face against the table saying;

"Nobody messes with my friends!"

It makes you think about the reality more differently. There is a difference between expansionism and protecting your ally.

Israel for instance I have said is not allowed in Syria as World general. No one is allowed in Syria but Russia who may be there to protect their ally. How am I to respond when Israel defies the World general saying that they have a right to be there to secure their national security? No you do not have a right to be there. No you may not interfere in Syria. The White hats are framing Assad with chemical weapons just before a UN envoy. Who are these white hats? The civilians of Aleppo claim the White helmets go around filming themselves saving people but they really only help their own rebel fighters and seldom help civilians. They claim to be 1st responders when there is calamity. Whenever food would arrive to help east Aleppo the white helmets would take it from the people and steal it all to themselves and give the people nothing to eat. The propaganda favors them in the media but on the ground they are middle men who deprive the people from aid. A munitions workshop would attempt to hide inside of hospitals where the white helmets make shells and bombs. Time after time they only save the rebels and leave civilians to die. Sometimes they sell body parts and organs from civilians to the Turkish. Walking around they film themselves for media stunts. Obviously there is an agenda to overthrow Assad. For control of oil or a strategic edge on Russia's back door we find ourselves facing down the barrel of World War III as a planet. The NATO drills encroaching Russia are some of the biggest in history. Who controls the World when NATO who is comprised of a conglomerate of superpower nations is acting like a bully on the World stage? Some say it is because Russia is one of the few nations left not yet under the financial control of the central bank. All the weapons in the World however we cannot allow to be mightier than this book. The pen must be mightier than the sword or we live in an Idiocracy.

We must again live in a World where people are able to read and write not just play video games. I speak for my generation when I say that we are apathetic about our power. We are taught that we are powerless. We are taught not to have a big ego and not to think too much of ourselves less we be called a narcissist. I refuse to believe that having no ego is the answer to our problems. It is perhaps by design that it is a sign of being spiritually evolved in the new age movement. You wouldn't want the people to think too much of themselves or they might want to take over. If they have better ideas they must be deemed irrelevant with their personal character attached to the fact that it is more important to belittle him and make him small again so we may all feel at ease about being utterly powerless.

It is paramount at this time we inform the public of the basics of social engineering. The people must understand how propaganda works and how they are socially manipulated to be distracted with mundane topics. In a mysterious video about Illumicorp they call the distraction with sports and celebrities "Infotainment."

The idea is to distract the public with a two party system and gossip stories so they will never rise up.

Perhaps when a comedian goes too far telling people the truth like George Carlin he gets the heart attack gun.

Perhaps when Robin Williams gets too political he gets hung on a door in a fake suicide.

The darker side to propaganda is perhaps the cold blooded killings of prominent public figures who start to get too many fans or too much common sense and reason starts to slip through the cracks.

Martain Luther King although we have a holiday for him in School we have to consider that it was found that he was killed by the government in a civil trial by the King family in 1999 where a jury found US government agencies and others guilty of assassinating MLK in Memphis 1968. 70 witnesses including Loyd Jowers who assisted the sniper and owned Jim's Grill where the shot was fired from it consisted of. We find James Earl Ray who we were told fired the shot had nothing to do with it. The 20th special forces group was instead shown to have been on location during King's murder.

If the average person understood the US government killed our greatest nonviolent civil rights leader in history would then people finally demand a change in government? The only move the government has left is to act like it never happened. Omitting things is something America does best. If the death of MLK can be hidden so well for so long why not hide an entire revolution on the West coast? They can try. They do a pretty good job. Who has heard about there being a new country? This book may be the 1st time you noticed. It will likely be the same for fellow Cascadians as well. Everyone is ignorant about something. I didn't see a Doug flag flying at random until driving up to Mt. Baker. It made my day. I went up the Nooksack and learned about how important this river is for still having 5 different kinds of Salmon. Our rivers in the northwest are not a slow moving stream filled with plastic garbage. Not yet. Not as long as I am president. It won't stay that way long however if you don't think I exist.

Most people don't believe in Sasquatch.

Most people don't believe in UFOs.

Most people don't believe Cascadia exists.

Everyone who cares for this land...

We are the Kings and Queens of Cascadia.

If I truly care for the planet more than anyone else does I am like the King of Earth.

It is a state of mind I want to share with you.

No one can take it away from you.

No one can tell me I'm not a Cascadian.

Not America. Not a random troll. Not my family.

Not anybody...

However humans have a problem when it comes to communication. No political representative has ever dared respond to me in the numerous times I have informed them of the new government. Why would they? Would you want to hear that you are out of a job? It is easier to call the World's smartest man a crack pot when your job is on the line.

If you don't believe me note that we would not even have web cams today if it weren't for the fact that Scientists at Cambridge wanted to check the level of their coffee pot. That's right folks... The incentive wasn't even to use the technology to communicate it was because something got between people and their coffee.

When I tell you that the Toll roads are illegal do you march on them to make a stink? No. The true spirit of the Boston tea party is dead and you are willing to just bend over and take another big fee or a big fine from big brother. How about a big glove up your butt to make sure you don't have anything in there? You will accept that glove because it's easier to pretend like this is liberty than it is to believe a nation could leave the union from America.

Arson Attacks from a Superpower

Jimmi Hendrix said: "When the power of love overcomes the love over power the World will know peace."

While the World turns a blind eye our new nation is on fire.

As a music artist I call myself GHOST PERSON because I am allot like a living ghost. Customer service ignores me and helps the person after me like I am not even there sometimes. As the Noocracy I am ignored because it is pompous to declare yourself the World's smartest person. It is arrogant and foolish to the average person. Yes but a government built on wisdom and intelligence as its foundation isn't this something we all desire? In our popularity contest of elections do we ever consider if the person running is the wisest and most intelligent?

We do not assume to think Donald Trump is the World's wisest and most intelligent person in spite his high IQ score. Trump makes mistakes like offering condolences for the wrong mass shooting referring to Texas instead of California.

I do not have this attitude that we should impeach Trump like some people do. I helped put him in office in a way by asking Wikileaks to dig something up on Clinton knowing she was going to start World War III with Russia. Certainly you would want to uncover something like Pizza gate to stop World War III. There is this ping pong of Republicans and Democrats however. We see Trump and Clinton shaking hands smiling before the election. Apparently they are on the same team. Ivanka and Chelsa Clinton are good friends for example. Mike Pence would be president. That is not good if Mike Pence is on camera talking about how he models after Dick Cheney as his highest inspiration. We could all be wishing we had an influence during a dog and pony show where all presidents are pre-selected. Consider that I got my way. Perhaps the World's smartest man does have an influence after all.

It is a government that does best to ignore me in public. If there is bilateral communication Cascadia might have to actually exist officially. America has to decide if it wants to face embarrassment in the spirit of its founders by acknowledging Cascadian independence or if it wants to occupy Cascadia in their wake in disgrace.

America has come a long way since its inception.

FEMA can now be seen in a room talking to law enforcement and firefighters attempting to explain that the founding fathers were terrorists.

He explains The founding fathers systematically had British officials assassinated and this is why they teach this. The British had certain political influence in certain pockets of the United States and George Washington issued death certificates for each of those officials. The British wanted to divide and conquer.

The divide and conquer strategy.

People can be divided over petty reasons. They say never to talk about politics at the dinner table. It divides families. Talking about redistribution of wealth on a bike ride on Devils gulch with my Uncle Keith I drew his contempt when saying that it might be ok to distribute the wealth of the top 1 to 3% back to the people. To say a man couldn't keep what he earns is nearly fighting words. I understand now the middle way is to allow for a living wage to be provided by donation. You must simply agree and say that Taxation is theft. It is theft...

However we can still provide for the lower class to circulate the economy by donation. We must eliminate this discrepancy to eliminate future class warfare. The rich and poor must never fight in the 1st place by providing a government that understands redistribution of wealth on a bell curve by donation. Every aspect of government must be or the market will not be free.

When does the government notice you have started a new country?

The government it's self being part of the Idiocracy for its failure to look after public safety over special interests is not quite as dumb as the public.

As the Noocracy I could be face to face at odds with a confused powerful government for years before the public catches on.

I stepped outside my camper and I remembered seeing my neighbor's house on fire. Three red fire trucks were putting the flames out. It always crosses my mind. Was that some kind of message for me personally? Is this another form of intimidation? Oddly the fire was never reported in the news that I could see. I'm a news hound. I always know what's going on and I am always responding to news stories in public claiming to be 1st president of the northwest.

On a daily basis I am trying to teach the public about basic rights.

Thomas Jefferson said; Educate and inform the whole mass of the people. They are the only sure reliance for the preservation of our liberty.

I find it difficult as he must of felt to inform and educate the public about basic rights. It becomes redundant and doing so has become all that I am. How else can we value our government again? If the police are shooting our dogs because they don't know how to deal with scary dogs and if they are shooting our friends and family it is our duty to inform the majority the truth that the government was never supposed to have this type of authority. If we are to make the deaths to gain independence from the British mean anything if we ourselves do not uphold the rights Jefferson was talking about.

I want to talk about fire now.

When your new nation is attacked with fire do you respond with fire or water?

If I am to be called wise I want it to be for this question.

If you are Darth Vader and you strike down Obi-Wan Kenobi what happens?

You lose.

History will side with the man who used water to fight back. This is why I ask for the World's largest firefighting fleet in history. A true Jedi uses water to fight back. Bruce Lee said be like water.

"You must be shapeless, formless, like water. When you pour water in a cup, it becomes the cup. When you pour water in a bottle, it becomes the bottle. When you pour water in a teapot, it becomes the teapot. Water can drip and it can crash. Become like water my friend."

I am not afraid of America.

I am fearless.

If you attack me like America was attacked on 9-11 I will react differently. I will call out instead those truly responsible instead of following through with the conspiracy to dominate the middle east with kinetic retaliation. America must learn to keep it's cool.

You don't just wave a flag and kill an old enemy if America doesn't understand what is going on.

Going after Saddam after 9-11 made America look like either a cunning Fox or an a blindfolded Idiot with a sword staggering after a flaming donkey tail. There were no weapons of mass destruction. Did you catch the people behind 9-11? No you did not. George W. Bush was coercing a classroom to give the impression that he was just twiddling his thumbs the morning of September 11th.

These are bold moves.

I often wonder about George H W Bush talking before the UN about how "It's a big idea. A New World Order."

One is left to wonder who's New World order?

What does the Noocracy think of the United Nations?

I think that there should be no World government only a World ARMY. A World government is too much to ask. You cannot expect every nation to bend to the same will. No matter what World government you create there will be a serious resistance movement and it will eventually fail.

A World ARMY is simple. The end of national rivalry is more important. Stomping out intentional ecological terrorism is important globally. Facing terrorism as a planet is not such a bad thing. We must always adapt.

The ambiguity of national rivalry is a headache. We will certainly destroy ourselves without my intervention. This intervention is brought to you by not only the World's brightest mind but a UFO summoner and extraterrestrials as well. There is good out there in the universe. As much as it may seem appealing in Hollywood movies to galvanize a World ARMY to defeat the hostile aliens I am here to tell you that whoever they are... they are nice so far.

They might blow up a Space X Rocket with a Facebook satellite.

We have to collectively wonder why they did it now.

Why do you think aliens blew up the Facebook rocket?

It was called an "Anomaly" on the launch pad.

If I had to guess they either thought it was an ICBM or it is because the Noocracy is being compartmentalized socially.

Certainly ultra-evolved star visitors are wanting to actually get their message out in a meaningful way.

Rockets create fire...

Extraterrestrials probably also see that we have discovered fire when we test nuclear bombs.

Nuclear bombs have been known to destroy other planets. Sometimes star visitors intervene when unsuitable leaders have control of the bomb. The CIA might be much the same way. Am I trying to say that it's time to eliminate Kim Jong Un? No I am not. He is simply intimidated after the Korean War and we must be careful because he claims to have the H-Bomb. North Korean missiles have already reached Alaska undetonated. America is nervous. The North Koreans have striven their entire lives from birth to be ready to fight what they see is an evil power.

Star visitors have written in a crop circle in Latin the words:

 "We oppose cunning and deceit"

We must not ignore these wise words from our extraterrestrial friends. If star visitors oppose those who are cunning I may have a powerful ally.

What is the most cunning way to attack a new nation?

Liz FitzGerald witnesses what might be a good example.

A small group of kids form Vancouver are seen throwing smoke bombs near the Columbia river.

"I saw this boy lob a smoke bomb down into the ravine," she said via phone Tuesday night. "I saw his friend or a guy that was there with him videotaping it with his phone. I looked over, and I said, 'Do you realize how dangerous that is?'"

We are lead to believe that this incident is just some random kids being irresponsible but as the Noocracy I question more deeply when I see that it is "Cascadian Locks" on fire.

Shortly before the Las Vegas shooting I talked about New Country not being as good as old cowboy songs and I have to wonder if there is some relation.

Before Kimbo Slice died I posted a video of him and Michael Jai White teaching him how to punch and in a short amount of time he was dead. I am left to wonder if there is any relation. I always wonder if it is a coincidence or the CIA heart attack gun telling me how fast they can kill people.

I had just been recently poisoned at my favorite place to eat at Rancho Chico on Division in Spokane where I also Ironically have my UFO photos hanging on the wall. I had once brought a UFO with my mind at that same intersection and posted it on the wall for people to see. I think what it could be about.

How can one Margarita nearly kill me over the next 8 days?

I didn't even have a meal.

It could be related to the UFO phenomenon.
Some people in the field have been known to mysteriously die.

It could be related to starting a new country here on the west coast.

Stanley Meyer we believe might have been killed by big oil at his favorite place to eat when his coffee was poisoned.

Why would big oil want to kill me?

I invented the Brisbine drive. I have made an over-unity drive by combining the right sized motor and generator. The idea is to create a motor that can create more electricity from it's counterpart generator.

In the 1980's you will see Stan Meyer on the news with his water powered car where he drove across America on 17 gallons of water. At the tail end you can hear the news lady say "The Pentagon is taking interest for use in tanks and military vehicles."

Only superficially is the NAVY really working on using water to power their ships. It is unfortunate. I think that even in the military the Idiocracy takes hold and when the idea sounds good when they access the man's patent they aren't actually always able to reproduce what the original inventor did.

Japan however is now openly making water powered cars. Japan like with electronics may lead the way with hydrogen we will see.

I think if the US really wanted me dead I would be dead. Why would you however want to kill the World's smartest man? Even the US has to consider that I may be important for one reason or another perhaps I have even saved the World before with the assistance of extraterrestrials. If I were the government I would be more concerned about them than me. I have a rap song where I mention that if you kill me then the aliens attack.

In a way I am mankind's last hope for human control of the planet. The way that we treat the World must change. We cannot simply clear cut it and burn it and spoil all its it's land and water. Some feel it is too late. I am more optimistic. If you don't have hope you have nothing but apathy and despair. We have to believe that we can do better. We have to believe that we can clean the Pacific garbage patch and recycle it. Our generation has to be more in tune than the Donald Trump generation. I wouldn't wish coal on my worst enemy I like to say.

On the topic of having an enemy I don't.

The Russians are not my enemy.

Al Qaeda is not my enemy.

The Islamic State is not my enemy.

Whoever it is…   Whoever is the bad guy is supposed to be.

Always be very careful not to have an enemy. If you are a nation and you say that you have on and name who they are you have just contributed to the downfall of your own nation.

It is always better to be for something than against something.

I am not Anti-American I am Pro Cascadian!

We don't burn the American flag we wave our own!

People who burn the American flag don't understand revolution. Violent protesters do not yet understand revolution.

Revolution is in the mind! It is a state of mind.

It is a Cascadian state of mind!

I protect America just by protecting the west coast. They are getting off easy. We work together in a way. As the Noocracy I give the US NAVY advice like using Laser Activated Weapons systems instead of THAAD missile systems because missiles intimidate other nations and are inferior at shooting them down compared to beam weapons. Of course like Einstein I will attempt to do what's best to protect the World from a loose cannon nations like Germany even if it becomes the US its self.

Cascadia is integral to America's national security at this point because if our new nation does not exist the US is in grave danger of being attacked for its foreign nation building and War history. If it doesn't learn to behave like everyone else I am going to reprimand it as the Noocracy like a parent would a child. These children and their nationalism must learn to get along. I would be wary of the snake oil salesmen who then are the 1st to sell you a global government. The 1st person I heard to mention the idea of a Global citizen was Bill Gates the eugenics philanthropist. I try to overlook to see the good in this man but will always have a hard time with a person playing god with the human population on Earth if I am to be a steward of it myself. Without windows would I even have this opportunity to write about him? I can groan about what I would do with someone else's money to help the homeless crisis but it gets you nowhere in life. In my book I will just groan to you the helpless reader.

This is a redress of grievances pending a petition of unsuspecting half-wits. redress of grievances is the right to make a complaint to, or seek the assistance of, one's government, without fear of punishment or reprisals.

I certainly have a right to complain after you burned down Cascadian Fruit shippers in Wenatchee, Washington America.

You did it didn't you...

You probably burn my home town all the time. It's just asking to get burned isn't it?

We know about lightning causing fires.

But this is the age of weather weapons. Lightning storms
perhaps are generated. You have to wonder because this is after
Tesla.

WENATCHEE Diane Reed stood amid the still-smoldering ash
and rubble of what used to be the family home Monday in the
affluent Broadview subdivision northwest of town.

"It reminds me of a war zone," said Reed, a substitute teacher
and mother of two girls.

TWISP, WashingtonThe largest fire in state history swept
through the eastern slopes of the Cascade Range with explosive
force last summer. The Carlton Complex fire burned more than
250,000 acres, devouring everything in its path at the hypersonic
pace of 3.8 acres a second.

Megafires can be spurred after cooking an area of the globe with
megawatts of electricity preventing the condensation cycle.

Think about it… As soon as I leave the union it is suddenly the
driest it has ever been on the West coast. Each summer is filled
with fires and there is no one seems to care much even after
choking on the smoke for 3 months strait. It has an effect on our
cities. The people slowly go ill and get headaches, dry noses and
respiratory problems. People don't care even when their
country is burning down they are so complacent. They will
smoke a cig through their N-95 filter mask. To me our firefighting
is superficial. I see our firefighters starting more fires than I see
them putting them out. Something is wrong not only with the
way we fight fires across the board but the intent behind
firefighting is not as genuine as it once was.

The Paradise fire burned the Olympic rain forest for the 1st time
in history. The American West from California to Alaska is our
territory beyond the Bio-region.

Olympic National Park — which occupies much of the Olympic Peninsula just west of Seattle — just endured its driest spring in over 100 years and a winter snow pack that was a mere 14 percent of average, according to the Park Service.

A recent episode of *The HAARP Report*, which tracks the activities of the U.S. military's "High Frequency Auroral Research Program" (which the federal government falsely claims has been shut down), provides five pieces of compelling evidence from recently captured satellite imagery that points to deliberate weather modification as the cause of California's drought.

You may have heard Ted Gunderson once head of the LA FBI talk about chemtrails regarding them as "Chemical death dumps" before being poisoned with arsenic.

"Chemtrails create a hot air layer at 30,000 feet, capping inversion," explains the report.

The 1st summer after I started the nation state was 2015…

Low pressure areas out in the Pacific Ocean that would normally move in a counterclockwise direction have been detected moving in an anomalous clockwise direction. *The HAARP Report*, highlighting exclusive imagery captured on April 10, 2015, shows a "burst" of clockwise, high pressure cloud movement that would never occur naturally, and that clearly suggests weather manipulation activity meant to break up cloud formation and prevent precipitation.

On a fire map can be seen so many fires at once and so many showing up at random sometimes 14 at a time one might think talking to those kids about their smoke bombs might be a good idea at this point. Certainly I could get to the bottom of all this right?

Well they are so young their names are being protected…

2) After breaking up the areas of low pressure that would have produced rain for California, HAARP's weather weaponry and associated chemtrails generate areas of very dry air that, under normal circumstances, would be humid. Satellite imagery captured in the days following April 10 show this dry air sitting stagnant rather than rotating, breaking up the potential formation of thunderstorms.

3) As it turns out, HAARP's weather manipulation machines can only operate when the D layer in the ionosphere has formed, which occurs after the sun has been up for three or four hours and ends in the evening. In the video, *The HAARP Report* shows how a storm that starts to pop up during this window of time is literally pushed to the right and destroyed. Dry air is pressed down, and once again the center is not moving in a counterclockwise direction as it should.

4) Looking again at a massive area of dry air brought about by HAARP and chemtrails, the report points out how satellite imagery of a ring of rising air and a central column of falling air captured at 10 a.m. in California on April 9 proves that a HAARP downburst sent high pressure descending air into the jet stream, once again preventing rain.

5) As this air descends, it just keeps getting bigger and bigger in the satellite imagery. And as it begins to reform, another HAARP downburst is observed on the north side of the front, with a signature clockwise flow around a high pressure area as it's sent downward. Put simply, the developing storm was basically broken up by HAARP, where it later reformed around Mexico and sent rain over New Mexico and Texas rather than California.

"Don't think for a minute that this drought in California is natural. They're using a variety of techniques to maintain this drought," warns *The HAARP Report*.

HAARP is an interesting and multifaceted topic.

There is a broad list of patents worth printing:

0462795 – July 16, 1891 – Method Of Producing Rain-Fall

1103490 – August 6, 1913 – Rain-Maker

1225521 – September 4, 1915 – Protecting From Poisonous Gas In Warfare

1338343 – April 27, 1920 – Process And Apparatus For The Production of Intense Artificial Clouds, Fogs, or Mists

1619183 – March 1, 1927 – Process of Producing Smoke Clouds From Moving Aircraft

1665267 – April 10, 1928 – Process of Producing Artificial Fogs

1892132 – December 27, 1932 – Atomizing Attachment For Airplane Engine Exhausts

1928963 – October 3, 1933 – Electrical System And Method

1957075 – May 1, 1934 – Airplane Spray Equipment

2097581 – November 2, 1937 – Electric Stream Generator – Referenced in 3990987

2409201 – October 15, 1946 – Smoke Producing Mixture

2476171 – July 18, 1945 – Smoke Screen Generator

2480967 – September 6, 1949 – Aerial Discharge Device

2550324 – April 24, 1951 – Process For Controlling Weather

2582678 – June 15, 1952 – Material Disseminating Apparatus For Airplanes

2614083 – October 14, 1952 – Metal Chloride Screening Smoke Mixture

2633455 – March 31, 1953 – Smoke Generator

2688069 – August 31, 1954 – Steam Generator – Referenced in 3990987

2721495 – October 25, 1955 – Method And Apparatus For Detecting Minute Crystal Forming Particles Suspended in a Gaseous Atmosphere

2730402 – January 10, 1956 – Controllable Dispersal Device

2801322 – July 30, 1957 – Decomposition Chamber for Monopropellant Fuel – Referenced in 3990987

2881335 – April 7, 1959 – Generation of Electrical Fields

2908442 – October 13, 1959 – Method For Dispersing Natural Atmospheric Fogs And Clouds

2986360 – May 30, 1962 – Aerial Insecticide Dusting Device

2963975 – December 13, 1960 – Cloud Seeding Carbon Dioxide Bullet

3126155 – March 24, 1964 – Silver Iodide Cloud Seeding Generator

3127107 – March 31, 1964 – Generation of Ice-Nucleating Crystals

3131131 – April 28, 1964 – Electrostatic Mixing in Microbial Conversions

3174150 – March 16, 1965 – Self-Focusing Antenna System

3234357 – February 8, 1966 – Electrically Heated Smoke Producing Device

3274035 – September 20, 1966 – Metallic Composition For Production of Hydroscopic Smoke

3300721 – January 24, 1967 – Means For Communication Through a Layer of Ionized Gases

3313487 – April 11, 1967 – Cloud Seeding Apparatus

3338476 – August 29, 1967 – Heating Device For Use With Aerosol Containers

3410489 – November 12, 1968 – Automatically Adjustable Airfoil Spray System With Pump

3429507 – February 25, 1969 – Rainmaker

3432208 – November 7, 1967 – Fluidized Particle Dispenser

3441214 – April 29, 1969 – Method And Apparatus For Seeding Clouds

3445844 – May 20, 1969 – Trapped Electromagnetic Radiation Communications System

3456880 – July 22, 1969 – Method Of Producing Precipitation From The Atmosphere

3518670 June 30, 1970 – Artificial Ion Cloud

3534906 – October 20, 1970 – Control of Atmospheric Particles

3545677 – December 8, 1970 – Method of Cloud Seeding

3564253 – February 16, 1971 – System And Method For Irradiation Of Planet Surface Areas

3587966 – June 28, 1971 – Freezing Nucleation

3601312 – August 24, 1971 – Methods of Increasing The Likelihood oF Precipitation By The Artificial Introduction Of Sea Water Vapor Into The Atmosphere Winward Of An Air Lift Region

3608810 – September 28, 1971 – Methods of Treating Atmospheric Conditions

3608820– September 20, 1971 – Treatment of Atmospheric Conditions by Intermittent Dispensing of Materials Therein

3613992 – October 19, 1971 – Weather Modification Method

3630950 – December 28, 1971 – Combustible Compositions For Generating Aerosols, Particularly Suitable For Cloud Modification And Weather Control And Aerosolization Process

USRE29142 – May 22, 1973 – Combustible compositions for generating aerosols, particularly suitable for cloud modification and weather control and aerosolization process

3659785 – December 8, 1971 – Weather Modification Utilizing Microencapsulated Material

3666176 – March 3, 1972 – Solar Temperature Inversion Device

3677840 – July 18, 1972 – Pyrotechnics Comprising Oxide of Silver For Weather Modification Use

3722183 – March 27, 1973 – Device For Clearing Impurities From The Atmosphere

3769107 – October 30, 1973 – Pyrotechnic Composition For Generating Lead Based Smoke

3784099 – January 8, 1974 – Air Pollution Control Method

3785557 – January 15, 1974 – Cloud Seeding System

3795626 – March 5, 1974 – Weather Modification Process

3808595 – April 30, 1974 – Chaff Dispensing System

3813875 – June 4, 1974 – Rocket Having Barium Release System to Create Ion Clouds In The Upper Atmosphere

3835059 – September 10, 1974 – Methods of Generating Ice Nuclei Smoke Particles For Weather Modification And Apparatus Therefore

3835293 – September 10, 1974 – Electrical Heating Apparatus For Generating Super Heated Vapors

3877642 – April 15, 1975 – Freezing Nucleant

3882393 – May 6, 1975 – Communications System Utilizing Modulation of The Characteristic Polarization of The Ionosphere

3896993 – July 29, 1975 – Process For Local Modification of Fog And Clouds For Triggering Their Precipitation And For Hindering The Development of Hail Producing Clouds

3899129 – August 12, 1975 – Apparatus for generating ice nuclei smoke particles for weather modification

3899144 – August 12, 1975 – Powder contrail generation

3940059 – February 24, 1976 – Method For Fog Dispersion

3940060 – February 24, 1976 – Vortex Ring Generator

3990987 – November 9, 1976 – Smoke generator

3992628 – November 16, 1976 – Countermeasure system for laser radiation

3994437 – November 30, 1976 – Broadcast dissemination of trace quantities of biologically active chemicals

4042196 – August 16, 1977 – Method and apparatus for triggering a substantial change in earth characteristics and measuring earth changes

RE29,142 – February 22, 1977 – Combustible compositions for generating aerosols, particularly suitable for cloud modification and weather control and aerosolization process

4035726 – July 12, 1977 – Method of controlling and/or improving high-latitude and other communications or radio wave surveillance systems by partial control of radio wave et al

4096005 – June 20, 1978 – Pyrotechnic Cloud Seeding Composition

4129252 – December 12, 1978 – Method and apparatus for production of seeding materials

4141274 – February 27, 1979 – Weather modification automatic cartridge dispenser

4167008 – September 4, 1979 – Fluid bed chaff dispenser

4347284 – August 31, 1982 – White cover sheet material capable of reflecting ultraviolet rays

4362271 – December 7, 1982 – Procedure for the artificial modification of atmospheric precipitation as well as compounds with a dimethyl sulfoxide base for use in carrying out said procedure

4402480 – September 6, 1983 – Atmosphere modification satellite

4412654 – November 1, 1983 – Laminar microjet atomizer and method of aerial spraying of liquids

4415265 – November 15, 1983 – Method and apparatus for aerosol particle absorption spectroscopy

4470544 – September 11, 1984 – Method of and Means for weather modification

4475927 – October 9, 1984 – Bipolar Fog Abatement System

4600147 – July 15, 1986 – Liquid propane generator for cloud seeding apparatus

4633714 – January 6, 1987 – Aerosol particle charge and size analyzer

4643355 – February 17, 1987 – Method and apparatus for modification of climatic conditions

4653690 – March 31, 1987 – Method of producing cumulus clouds

4684063 – August 4, 1987 – Particulates generation and removal

4686605 – August 11, 1987 – HAARP Patent / EASTLUND PATENT – Method and apparatus for altering a region in the earth's atmosphere, ionosphere, and/or magnetosphere

4704942 – November 10, 1987 – Charged Aerosol

4712155 – December 8, 1987 – Method and apparatus for creating an artificial electron cyclotron heating region of plasma

4744919 – May 17, 1988 – Method of dispersing particulate aerosol tracer

4766725 – August 30, 1988 – Method of suppressing formation of contrails and solution therefor

4829838 – May 16, 1989 – Method and apparatus for the measurement of the size of particles entrained in a gas

4836086 – June 6, 1989 – Apparatus and method for the mixing and diffusion of warm and cold air for dissolving fog

4873928 – October 17, 1989 – Nuclear-sized explosions without radiation

4948257 – August 14, 1990 – Laser optical measuring device and method for stabilizing fringe pattern spacing

1338343– August 14, 1990 – Process and Apparatus for the production of intense artificial Fog

4999637 – March 12, 1991 – Creation of artificial ionization clouds above the earth

5003186 – March 26, 1991 – Stratospheric Welsbach seeding for reduction of global warming

5005355 – April 9, 1991 – Method of suppressing formation of contrails and solution therefor

5038664 – August 13, 1991 – Method for producing a shell of relativistic particles at an altitude above the earths surface

5041760 – August 20, 1991 – Method and apparatus for generating and utilizing a compound plasma configuration

5041834 – August 20, 1991 – Artificial ionospheric mirror composed of a plasma layer which can be tilted

5056357 – October 15, 1991- Acoustic method for measuring properties of a mobile medium

5059909 – October 22, 1991 – Determination of particle size and electrical charge

5104069 – April 14, 1992 – Apparatus and method for ejecting matter from an aircraft

5110502 – May 5, 1992 – Method of suppressing formation of contrails and solution therefor

5156802 – October 20, 1992 – Inspection of fuel particles with acoustics

5174498 – December 29, 1992 – Cloud Seeding

5148173 – September 15, 1992 – Millimeter wave screening cloud and method

5242820 - September 7, 1993 – Army Mycoplasma Patent Patent

5245290 – September 14, 1993 – Device for determining the size and charge of colloidal particles by measuring electroacoustic effect

5286979 – February 15, 1994 – Process for absorbing ultraviolet radiation using dispersed melanin

5296910 – March 22, 1994 – Method and apparatus for particle analysis

5327222 – July 5, 1994 – Displacement information detecting apparatus

5357865 – October 25, 1994 – Method of cloud seeding

5360162 – November 1, 1994 – Method and composition for precipitation of atmospheric water

5383024 – January 17, 1995 – Optical wet steam monitor

5425413 – June 20, 1995 – Method to hinder the formation and to break-up overhead atmospheric inversions, enhance ground level air circulation and improve urban air quality

5434667 – July 18, 1995 – Characterization of particles by modulated dynamic light scattering

5441200 – August 15, 1995 – Tropical cyclone disruption

5486900 – January 23, 1996 – Measuring device for amount of charge of toner and image forming apparatus having the measuring device

5556029 – September 17, 1996 – Method of hydrometeor dissipation (clouds)

5628455 – May 13, 1997 – Method and apparatus for modification of supercooled fog

5631414 – May 20, 1997 – Method and device for remote diagnostics of ocean-atmosphere system state

5639441 – June 17, 1997 – Methods for fine particle formation

5762298 – June 9, 1998 – Use of artificial satellites in earth orbits adaptively to modify the effect that solar radiation would otherwise have on earth's weather

5800481 – September 1, 1998 – Thermal excitation of sensory resonances

5912396 – June 15, 1999 – System and method for remediation of selected atmospheric conditions

5922976 – July 13, 1999 – Method of measuring aerosol particles using automated mobility-classified aerosol detector

5949001 – September 7, 1999 – Method for aerodynamic particle size analysis

5984239 – November 16, 1999 – Weather modification by artificial satellite

6025402 – February 15, 2000 – Chemical composition for effectuating a reduction of visibility obscuration, and a detoxifixation of fumes and chemical fogs in spaces of fire origin

6030506 – February 29, 2000 – Preparation of independently generated highly reactive chemical species

6034073 – March 7, 2000 – Solvent detergent emulsions having antiviral activity

6045089 – April 4, 2000 – Solar-powered airplane

6056203 – May 2, 2000 – Method and apparatus for modifying supercooled clouds

6110590 – August 29, 2000 – Synthetically spun silk nanofibers and a process for making the same

6263744 – July 24, 2001 – Automated mobility-classified-aerosol detector

6281972 – August 28, 2001 – Method and apparatus for measuring particle-size distribution

6315213 – November 13, 2001 – Method of modifying weather

6382526 – May 7, 2002 – Process and apparatus for the production of nanofibers

6408704 – June 25, 2002 – Aerodynamic particle size analysis method and apparatus

6412416 – July 2, 2002 – Propellant-based aerosol generation devices and method

6520425 – February 18, 2003 – Process and apparatus for the production of nanofibers

6539812 – April 1, 2003 – System for measuring the flow-rate of a gas by means of ultrasound

6553849 – April 29, 2003 – Electrodynamic particle size analyzer

6569393 – May 27, 2003 – Method And Device For Cleaning The Atmosphere

0056705 A1 – March 17, 2005 – Weather Modification by Royal Rainmaking Technology

6890497 – May 10, 2005 – Method For Extracting And Sequestering Carbon Dioxide

7965488 – November 9, 2007 – Methods Of Removing Aerosols From The Atmosphere

8048309 – August 28, 2008 – Seawater-Based Carbon Dioxide Disposal

8012453 – October 27, 2008 – Carbon Sequestration And Production Of Hydrogen And Hydride

7645326 – January 12, 2010 – RFID environmental manipulation

7655193 – February 2, 2010 – Apparatus For Extracting And Sequestering Carbon Dioxide

8079545 – December 20, 2011 – Ground based Manipulation and Control of Aerial Vehicle during nonflying operations

0117003 – October 5, 2012 – Geoengineering Method Of Business Using Carbon Counterbalance Credits – alternate link

8373962 – February 12, 2013 – Charged seed cloud as a method for increasing particle collisions and for scavenging airborne biological agents and other contaminants

Among these patents consider that there are ways of geoengineering to create drought as well as flooding. If you have one you will likely expect to have the latter. So those are two things we as Cascadians should learn to adapt to. How can we make our plants grow with dwindling water?

An effort now to do things like root containment to save water will help us more in the long run. We have to take steps so water bottle companies don't guzzle our fresh water. If the currency is to be based on water we must protect it and if we are dealing with secret powers who have super weapons we must identify that and who and we must create options for a civilized diplomacy in their wake before we jump head first into rocking the boat. If the HAARP plays with nice we are talking about something that can potentially take out ICBMs like our space friends. However misuse has been predicted. If we could put rain in the desert and make it green that would be nice. It is a double edge sword that can evaporate and dry a new nation's crops to a crisp. It is a most devastating weapon in the wrong hands. Superheating the sky is not something the Idiocracy is ready for. They struggle to understand and mock the messenger. How can they understand it let alone galvanize to combat against super weapons? They cannot. The people have simply become cannon fodder to higher hands. The people would cower in fear if presented with such odds. Beam weapons torching the forest is not something the average Pokemon' player is going to think about. Governor Jesse Ventura outside the world of wrestling decided to wrestle the topic of HAARP by flying up to the gate and attempting to get access. He was declined and found it interesting a former governor wouldn't be able to tour the facility. With all that you can do it seems like something we should all make an effort to study if not physically dismantle if it gets out of hand. This would be something I could do with a World ARMY. Understanding the latest weapons is something we need to understand at least at the highest level nationally. Consolidating super weapons into one secretive international body that we can trust is important I believe. When I say secretive I say it because when you give the average joe on the street a super weapon they just might use it. As a true martial artist I feel that weapons are the tools of death and should not be admired and their use should not be so romantic. When the UN celebrates 70 years of peacekeeping I marvel at how brandishing lethal machine guns during a peacekeeping mission is going to garner more peace. These lethal weapons UN soldiers hold are a lethal weapon that intimidates. You would instead brandish non-lethal weapons if they were controlled by the Noocracy. Much like we have the problem with the mentality of the former US government in the west when they brandish lethal weapons as a government body this means they do not yet understand our unalienable right to life. People argue that the officer has a right to defend himself. Time and time again we have seen officers shoot unarmed people who were holding their wallet or even nothing at all. Paranoid government officials with guns shoot innocent people to a point where we fear the police more than a thief. When they are on the street people will suicide by cop knowing how trigger happy the police are. You instead have a more simple government where the people look after themselves and live shootings and lethal events are met by the Cascadian ARMY using state of the art nonlethal weapons. For every wolf that the former government wants to shoot to please paranoid cattle ranchers we will instead recruit that animal to our ranks in the Cascadian ARMY. I will bring them to the former governors house and get them to sit and shake hands and howl the great howl. I had a wolf. It was my quadriplegic brothers dog who took her all around Bellingham in his electric wheelchair. They can be tamed. Alex was the most human dog of all she would make sounds like Rooooar like she agreed with what you were talking about. She would sing along when I played sax and rolled the streets with me on roller skates. Do we really want people like Sarah Palin shooting them all? No we don't. Why not tranquilize them and move some to the Olympic forest where invasive mountain goats are ramming people with their heads! Isn't that what a responsible governor would do? It doesn't seem to matter if they are republican or democrat they are both shooting our wolves! Shooting the wolves and giving all our neighborhood's dogs antifreeze. Someone is doing it. We don't know if it is some wretched territorial man who hates dogs in his garage or if it's the former government. After fire and arson comes killing the animals we eat the animals that might protect our neighborhoods. Cops are train to shoot our dogs on sight if they even approach barking facing the officer.

I know how to handle scary dogs. We had a Pitbull named Elenor who was a tank bigger than any I had ever seen. If you were walking her you would find that she was actually walking you. You were along for the ride and if she saw a little dog yapping at her behind a fence she would floor it dragging your feet through the gravel. A Pit Bull can pull over a ton and they are strong. People like them for a reason. They protect the family. When an officer who is untrained with scary dogs shoots the family protector that doesn't feel like protection. Protect and serve. You walk up to the dog and slowly put your hand out for it to sniff. Then you get down on one knee and you let it sniff or lick your neck. You trust the dog... You let the dog have a free shot at your neck with the intent to? You must be crazy or you might just happen to understand how bad ass dogs work. Now the dog trusts you and it will defend you with its life. If you are chill with the family then the dog considers you part of the family. If you yell at someone in the family that dog is ready to kill you. If you grab a gun a dog that is trained will grab that gun before you can use it. The police know all about it. If they can handle German Shepard's so well why can't they handle a stranger's dog? They need to disband and go home. They need to quit their job and join my ARMY to be retrained. The police in UK don't kill someone with a knife. If you can't handle one guy with a knife without using lethal force you are a bunch of cowards and shills who fail to understand basic rights. You can't just fire on people in Cascadia. You can't set fires and just get away with it forever or the Noocracy will sniff you out. I will grow suspicious.

Troll hackers can become super investigators overnight. Nearly all of them smoke pot and they can flop government websites. If they can turn a news site into porn they can also post a meme that tells the truth about reality. At this point you have to answer to people who have already hacked NASA to find they have been hiding UFOs from the public. Gary McKinnon, who faced a 10-year fight against extradition to the US has found just that. Fire in the sky slowly shoots from space takes form and we are left to explain what it is when a meteor moves swiftly in contrast.

Many UFOs are now caught on footage and the scientific community has yet to take the field a seriously as the rest. The most important field of research in human history is left to those society have been socially engineered to think of as crack pots. Now with things like the Disclosure project are comprised of a variety of military and commercial pilots uniting to disclose the truth about the phenomenon. Tesla's death ray has become a reality in 2017. A rush to control space nationally has been going on since Sputnik. The international space station has brought nations together but every nation's current quest for dominance boosts their desire to have the upper hand in orbit. If the Americans have beam weapons in space well guess what... So do the Russians. I warn specifically for the future misuse of Asteroids as a weapon because large enough meteors dropped in to destroy cities can hurt life for all our planet if left unchecked. Without a World ARMY to hold nations accountable for their space weapons we are all in danger of our forests burning to beam weapons. Such weapons being used on Star visitors who have finally come to Earth all this way to be greeted with a deadly beam is the ultimate in man's stupidity. If we were to anger a benevolent race of aliens with our hostile knee jerk

response or for simply violating our air space one of these idiots
may trigger an intergalactic conflict where humans no longer
have control of the Earth. Let's be honest. We have been
irresponsible when you look at Fukushima. Even when the
Noocracy warns you years in advance no one hears him. To you
such warnings are those of a man in a tin foil hat who belongs in
the funny farm. But look what we have done. We have nearly
killed the ocean. We could alter the chemistry of the ocean and
kill life on our entire planet because we bludgeon our discoveries
like a sledge hammer on every unwitting species. We think we
are smart but to the Noocracy are seen as irresponsible Dotards.

When this generation of money grubbers finally gets to lavish
and swim in all their money in their 80s and 90s we will look back
and wonder why the planet didn't mean anything to them. We
will look back at that crazy Cascadian who talked about basic
rights never being upheld by the government. We will wonder
why I had no friends or support when people start dropping like
flies from the next live bio-weapon in their typical flu shots.

I ask an obvious question again. Why can we get a Trillion dollars
to make weapons of war to start fires but are strangely unable to
match that when it comes to putting them out? Why is selling
weapons such a strong point for America? Don't you want to
stop the perpetuation of armed conflict? How is providing the
World with weapons making the World a safer place? It is not.
There is this backward thinking that stay strong in the Idiocracy.
Double think should no longer exist. Peacekeeping should not
mean War on the ground. You can't fool me. You can't fool the
Noocracy. Eventually you have to decide if you want to silence
the whistleblowers or listen to what they have to say. If you
silence the whistle blowers and omit decent instead of having
communication with them about the topic in a public forum it is
you who are the cunning and deceitful.

If there is a terrorist you don't simply kill them. You see why they
are a terrorist. You address the core foundation of why the

attack is happening in the 1st place. If you refrain from doing so with the Bush attitude that "We don't negotiate with terrorists," You are doing a disservice to your people that could last generations where conflict happens and people don't necessarily even understand why they are getting bombed or why there is fire every summer like we have her in Cascadia. I seek dialogue with America in a public forum because I know that words are more powerful than weapons. If I am allowed no audience they win. The revolution will not be televised. Word of mouth movements however have a tenancy to crumble an empire from the ground up. For instance if you stack a pyramid of sugar cubes on a tray then fill the bottom with water. The entire pyramid will eventually dissolve from the ground up. A grass roots movement will have this affect. As long as there are people like me who claim to be Cascadian not American who were born here and die here we will have our revolution. My child will not have to stand for the pledge of allegiance at school if he doesn't want to. Even if public schools attempt to indoctrinate him to be American at home he will be Cascadian. The government likes to separate the children from their parents. The government wants to have that power to bus all the children to a place their parents will never find them on a whim. This is the danger we face. This divide and conquer tactic of dividing the children from their parents will break the spirit of the average family. People would feel helpless... as helpless as I do sometimes about facing the World's biggest super power. Already strange things are happening to lay the groundwork for types of separation. Children who do and do not have their vaccines if they will be allowed into school is one. Do you condone mandatory compulsory vaccination? Are you stupid enough to let your kid get vaccinated? Are you stupid enough to let them into public school? It is almost like this is how it is made up. Parents who are irresponsible to allow their children in public school where they have to be injected with a mysterious bio-weapon to get in perhaps the government feels such a parent would be unfit to raise them. Will you allow your child to come do our brainwashing mantra to god and country every morning? At first doing the pledge of allegiance children were made to do a Nazi style salute to the flag. This was changed to a hand over the heart. It was something to force more loyalty to the country.

I have no pledge of allegiance for Cascadia.

If you want to leave the country and be something else that is just fine with me. That is what freedom is all about. I was born here in The Cascadia bioregion though and I am more concerned about leadership in our area. It is fool hearty to think I can fix America even if I were its president. Any sitting US president doesn't have the power to make America change at the pace I require. So long as our representatives care more about profit than the will of the people it is a dangerous game. You cannot change America but you can break away and start a new country. In doing so will be the best thing you could do for it. We get to teach America why we started a new country and that will have an influence. Other states may also start their own country. This is really the way America was intended to be. Think of Cascadia more like the US having its 1st child. America and Canada had a baby. You wouldn't harm your own baby would you America? It's too late for an abortion. That would not be upholding our unalienable right to life! You don't get to abort Cascadia like you did the South. We are on the right side of history this time not you. When you battle with those on the right side of history you may win the battle but you will always lose the war. As World general I am beyond petty national disputes. Nations at war are now like children fighting in the eyes of the people of Earth. Let it stay that way. The days of fractured military leadership are over. The World will help me build my firefighting fleet if it believes me. We will perfect heavy lifting and bring back the airship. I would of put Alberta out with the greatest fleet ever made when the tar sands burned. I am not afraid to help Canada. I am a Cascadian. Neighborhoods should not look like they have been hit with a nuclear bomb this is not going to be Fallout Cascadia. We are not cooking up rad roaches on the open fire in this life time if I can help it.

Independence and the World ARMY

Cascadia as an idea has been around for half a century however little is known about Cascadia the nation even to insiders.

We gained our independence from the US July 1st 2014 under Adam Aleander Brisbine the Noocracy.

Our flag the Doug flag designed by Alexander Baretich.

I wrote the national anthem.

A good place to start is the documentary Occupied Cascadia.

Flyers are perhaps posted on a phone pole that say "US out of Cascadia!" The book Ecotopia talks about our pristine bioregion.

The Oregon Country and the Columbia District are precursors to Cascadia.

An 1813 letter from Thomas Jefferson to John Jacob Astor congratulated Astor on the establishment of Fort Astoria (the coastal fur trade post of Astor's Pacific Fur Company and described Fort Astoria as "the germ of a great, free, and independent empire on that side of our continent, and that liberty and self-government spreading from that as well as from this side, will insure their complete establishment over the whole."

He went on to criticize the British, who were also establishing fur trade networks in the region: "It would be an afflicting thing, indeed, should the English be able to break up the settlement. Their bigotry to the bastard liberty of their own country, and habitual hostility to every degree of freedom in any other, will induce the attempt." The same year of Jefferson's letter, Fort

Astoria was sold to the British North West Company, based in Montreal.

John Quincy Adams agreed with Jefferson's views about Fort Astoria, and labeled the entire Northwest as "the empire of Astoria", although he also saw the whole continent as "destined by Divine Providence to be peopled by one nation. As late as the 1820s James Monroe and Thomas Hart Benton thought the region west of the Rockies would be an independent nation.

Elements among the region's colonist population starting in the 1840s sought to form their own country, despite their small number. Oregon pioneer John McLoughlin was employed as the "Chief Factor" (regional administrator) by the Hudson's Bay Company for the Columbia District, administered from Fort Vancouver. McLoughlin was a significant force in the early history of the Oregon Country, and argued for its independence. In 1842 McLoughlin (through his lawyer) advocated an independent nation that would be free of the United States during debates at the Oregon Lyceum. This view won support at first and a resolution was adopted. When the first settlers of the Willamette Valley held a series of politically foundational meetings in 1843, called the "Wolf Meetings," a majority voted to establish an independent republic. Action was postponed by George Abernethy of the Methodist Mission to wait on forming an independent country.

In May 1843, the settlers in the Oregon Country created their first "western style" government as a Provisional Government. Several months later the Organic Laws of Oregon were drawn up to create a legislature, an executive committee, a judicial system, and a system of subscriptions to defray expenses. Members of the ultra-American party insisted that the final lines of the Organic Act would be "until such time as the USA extend their jurisdiction over us" to try to end the Oregon Territorial independence movement. George Abernethy was elected its first and only Provisional Governor, with an opposing faction led by

Osborne Russell favoring independence. Russell proposed that the Oregon Territory not join the United States, but instead become a Pacific Republic that stretched from the Pacific Ocean to the Continental Divide.

British claims north of the Columbia River were ceded to the United States by the contentious Oregon Treaty of 1846. In 1860, there were three different statements from separate influential individuals on the creation of a "Pacific Republic."

Cascadia in 2017 the nation state spans the entire west coast. At first I wanted California to be its own country as the Republic of California. I feel the same way about Governor Brown as Kate Brown and Jay Inslee. They all three have good intentions but have failed me in some major regard. When California got hit by its major drought we see a problem with too many people populating an area with too little water. LA isn't as sustainable as we are in the northwest. There is animosity for some Californians coming here due to a feeling that they are spoiled and rich. When William Shatner talked about how we could just make a big pipeline of fresh water to California we felt a little unsympathetic. We felt like California might run our rivers dry. But now I see the importance of irrigation. Irrigation is the 1st phase of true civilization and that water may be important for all of us considering California is a serious food producer. I fear for the almonds of California as they import more and more honey bees. If it is by design that Monsanto desires to decimate the honey bee to implement their own android pollinators to patent the entire food process we would be in dire straits. I think on the west coast it should be a national imperative to save the honey be and oust Monsanto and all its herbicide from our new nation. We must stand on the side of protecting nature and preserving the original DNA structure of our food. We need to bring the little guy back and amplify our food diversity by 100 fold.

I think of Ben Franklin's community garden.

We should be inspired by all that America has given us.

Here are the 13 Virtues of Ben Franklin:

Temperance: Eat not to Dullness, Drink not to elevation.

Silence: Speak not but what may benefit others or yourself.
Avoid trifling conversation.

Order: Let all your Things have their places. Let each part of your
Business have it time.

Resolution: Resolve to perform what you ought. Perform without
fail what you resolve.

Frugality: Make no expense but to do good to others or yourself
and waste nothing.

Industry: Lose no time. Be always employ'd in something useful.
Cut off all unnecessary actions.

Sincerity: Use no hurtful deceit. Think innocently and justly; and
if you speak speak accordingly.

Justice: Wrong none, by doing Injuries or omitting the benefits
that are your duty.

Moderation: Avoid extremes. Forbear resenting Injuries so much
that as you think they deserve.

Cleanliness Tolerate no Uncleanness in body, Clothes or
Habitation.

Tranquility: Be not disturbed at Trifles, or at accidents common
or unavoidable.

Chastity: Rarely use Venery but for Health or Offspring; never to Dullness, weakness or the injury of your own or another's peace or reputation.

Humility: Imitate Jesus and Socrates.

I will take it all this wisdom with a grain of salt.

I think what is important right now is getting people to overcome the taboo of the World's smartest person volunteering as president or leader. We need to get over the taboo of our own bodies. Cascadian law is not Sharia law. We are going to allow the Baristas to keep getting tips for their bikini because the government has no business telling the people what kind of clothes they can wear. It is wild that the government in the US could have become to encroaching that local officials think they can dictate what people can and cannot wear. The taboo of our own body we were born with can no longer be allowed to be taboo about breasts and genitalia. The Romans did their Olympics naked. Not to model after their society but think about how far it's gone. If you expose your god given body in public there is an authority who feels it is their moral right to put a person in a cage. I think of someone's mom I knew who spent all her time in bed complaining about things and forced her border collie to be in a tiny cage all day. This particular breed of dogs is known for being very agile and the most intelligent. We have to consider that the dog in this case may be smarter than its owner.

What gives the Idiocracy the moral authority to put the World's smartest man in a cage? It has none. The reality Americans must eventually face is that putting people in a cage for profit will put the nation on the wrong side of history. This type of encroaching police state cannot be accepted if we are to still believe in or understand liberty. The toll roads are simply police state checkpoints to an unwitting public. Active denial weapons perhaps are being set up all around us while we continue to vote like it matters in this charade. A pure democracy must be tempered with benevolent intelligence. A government for profit is no government at all as it's people become an afterthought and cannon fodder to corporate agendas to be dominant.

The public must rise up if there is an undeclared war being conducted without the consent of congress.

The public must rise up when confronted with the prospect of weather modification as a weapon.

The public must rise up when there becomes hidden weapons in our compulsory vaccines.

The public must rise up after failing to understand the government doesn't have the moral authority to execute or blow people's brains out with the police.

The public must rise up in the face of random arson attacks by the former government.

FEMA knows that Cascadia is rising when they have a web page talking about the big one pending in our subduction zone. The pun is intended. The former government acknowledges the Idiocracy and they want us to be prepared as a new nation.

The former government will continue to portray the west as America until the people are intelligent enough to understand they really live in Cascadia.

The public must rise above the Lemming effect where group think dictates the picture of the reality we live in instead of people who finally have a mind of their own.

Social engineering has made people who use the term Chemtrails a crazy person. They use language to discard the perspective of people in society. Perhaps they prefer the term Geoengineering. When you use a different term a different group of people are going to listen to you about the topic. There are other terms... There is hidden terminology.

The department of energy says: "Tropospheric aerosols."

The CIA says: "Stratospheric aerosol injections."

NASA says: "Solar radiation management"

The Albedo effect and Albedo modification...

Cloud whitening...

VPTRE.

Bill Vander Zalm, former Canadian Premier for British Columbia received a 40 page report from Ottowa that confirms a covert Chemtrails – Geoengineering operation is in progress.

To the average person we are talking about a phenomenon that they will claim is contrails not chemtrails. They will remain on that level and it will go no further. When you explain that you can identify them as trails that last longer than 3 minutes that fan out creating an overcast for the rest of the day it will go out the other ear.

The youth are indoctrinated to believe in a school textbook that such geoengineering is to combat climate change. The official cover is to combat climate change and so long as it seems as something good for the planet the Lemming will accept it as gospel.

Dennis Kucinich speaks of Chemtrails and HR 2977 – The "Space Preservation Act" before congress. We well could of used something like the Space preservation act to prevent what has become beam weapons in space run by nationalism.

"To preserve the cooperative, peaceful uses of space for the benefit of all humankind by permanently prohibiting the basing of weapons in space by the United States, and to require the President to take action to adopt and implement a world treaty banning space-based weapons."

Such exotic weapons in the initial write up included:

(i) electronic, psychotronic, or information weapons;

(ii) chemtrails;

(iii) high altitude ultra low frequency weapons systems;

(iv) plasma, electromagnetic, sonic, or ultrasonic weapons;

(v) laser weapons systems;

(vi) strategic, theater, tactical, or extraterrestrial weapons; and

(vii) chemical, biological, environmental, climate, or tectonic weapons.

You see the people who made this act are allot like me.

Perhaps they are privy to the fact that mankind has been blasting extraterrestrials in orbit with beam weapons. I have seen UFOs in orbit skirting away from such weapons.

Alfred Webre and Carol Rosin are heroes for trying to stop weapons in space from attacking star visitors. Who is allowing this kind of behavior? National governments playing god in orbit that is who. I am the real 1st Earth contact for the United Nations

Office for Outer Space Affairs regardless if I am on the payroll or not.

We should embody that spirit to prevent nations from playing god in orbit. We have come so far with the International Space Station. We ended the cold War essentially with the Russians in orbit. So why on the ground is all of NATO intimidating Russia with its drills? Earth needs leadership. Leadership in space that supersedes all national government agendas for dominance.

If beam weapons are scaring off space ships in orbit who traveled light years just get here that is not the type of welcome mat I had in mind for Earth. That is not something that is in the spirit of Carl Sagan and Voyager. We must inform people like Jeff Sessions that good people do smoke pot.

The Canadian government is fully aware that aircraft are spraying chemicals into the atmosphere.

Although the Canadian government denies responsibility for spraying, they claim to be monitoring the operation, according to Vander Zalm.

We don't have to acknowledge orbital weapons are picking on unsuspecting extraterrestrials but we can at least acknowledge chemtrails.

What match am I even as a great martial artist with my bow and arrow every morning against fire starting beam weapons? Words are our only weapon and until words mean something again will they every be able to galvanize nations to stop misbehavior in space or on the World stage.

Star visitors know that type of thing is happening but they also can read our minds and from any city they can pick out a person like me who is talking directly about them and their 1st impression of us.

When star visitors see how Israel treats the Palestinians or how villages are burnt in Africa when militants take over the see only once side of humanity.

Let's comb over the top genocides they might of witnessed:

The Holocaust...

General plan Ost

Holodomor

The Cambodian genocide

Kazakhstan famine of 1932-1933

Armenian Genocide

Rwandan genocide

Zunghar genocide

Circassian genocide

Serbian genocide

Bangladesh genocide

Greek genocide including the Pontic

Assyrian genocide

Albigensian Crusade

Aardakh

After listing them all you start to get a feeling like you live on a planet that has lost its way. How could these petty differences between us lead to so much death? Waving a flag for your nation and pride in your nation or race or religion should not allow us to stoop so low.

When World events are known to be witnessed by advanced civilizations in footage and photographs we owe it to ourselves to give them a better impression of our World and who we have become.

Just because we see fire in the sky doesn't mean we shoot at it.

We are not these same red necks who's answer to everything is just "Nuke em!" I am actually a Cascadian.

If Cascadians are going to be anything we are going to be smart and we are going to be survivors. Leading the World is not my cup of tea but I will if I feel no one is looking out for our longevity as a planet. My answer isn't just the urgency that Stephan Hawking has that we have to get off the planet as soon as possible. My answer is that if we want legitimate interstellar space travel when our planet is about to burn from the sun turning to a Red Giant that we have to come together as one Military or we are a danger to other planets. If we desire real communication with beings who are light years ahead of us we must 1st galvanize to make sure nations aren't shooting them in orbit like Red Necks. When we allow nations to shoot beam weapons at ships in orbit we are inviting our own destruction and takeover. Intellectually I already have. Physically and socially it may take generations for our planet to realize it hasn't been making all the right moves.

We have been lucky that we haven't got our butts stomped into the ground by superior life forms. When I see a meteor fly over a city I can only wonder at this stage if it is natural or a shot off the bow to some unwitting city below.

How can you start a new country in America without being the most powerful influence in the World? You cannot. It will kill you.

If only other Cascadians knew they are up against a brick wall like it's a WAL-MART human holding area near the train tracks. If there were suddenly shoot on sight orders for anyone who wasn't vaccinated or pinned up inside the building these fun loving flag waving soccer players in the northwest would run out of beer and realize they have no guns to fight back with.

We are at a crossroads when it comes to liberty and freedom.

If you fight with a bully you better be ready to win the fight.

Not a single Cascadian is ready for that fight. It's a fight they know they will lose. This is why it is seen as a post collapse society. For me however I am winning that fight with my mind in a book right now. Perhaps it will be a banned book. Some would rather shoot 1st than ask questions about the foundation of the country. When we shoot 1st like we do in orbit we bring the collapse of our own civilization. Perhaps some things are meant to collapse. Every nation in history has collapsed for one reason or another. It's leaders became too bold and cocky. When the World's most powerful nation gets too cocky it requires the Noocracy to rise up and a World ARMY to rival it. Genocide is too often overlooked. We turn a blind eye to it when it is not our nation and our own people. In the end however the people of the planet are one. The Noocracy must protect all people across all nations from genocide. Even if the richest most prevailing minds condone the idea of picking and choosing what impoverished nations get help and what ones do not we must rise above them. Wealth does not mean you are an ethical person. Most who have become wealthy got that way by subjugating others to labor. This is not the perspective of a person who believes in equality and basic rights. To them humans are simply a resource in a dehumanized world. To the rich people are born and live simply as their personal organ donors. We have to come to terms with the reality that there are rich people who like to kill stuff. When the Obama ban on imported trophy animals gets lifted so Donald Trump Jr. or someone else can bring home a Lion head or Elephant tusk don't be confused when they call this animal conservation. Killing animals that are endangered is never animal conservation. In the movie the Purge we see a sneak peek into a World that may already exist where the rich have an opportunity to hunt the poor. This is likely the their plan when they run out of animals to shoot. Perhaps a random Dentist Walter Palmer is killing Cecil the Lion for a selfie. Perhaps it makes some of us irked when we see Kendall Jones and it goes viral on Facebook but is that the full extent of it?

Kinessa Johnson from Yelm Washington working for the Veterans Empowered to Protect African Wildlife holds a sniper rifle like she is going to hunt down poachers and snipe them out but we are left to wonder if the entire thing is a front when finding out she has only done one tour as a motor pool mechanic. It sounds like a noble crusade on the surface. In the end there may be fronts for doing good deeds just for show. Would killing the poachers be upholding their unalienable right to life? At this point we see the slippery slope towards dehumanization when we say that it's ok to shoot them outright. Certainly something needs to be done though. An international body to protect endangered species with nonlethal weapons is more in order. In spite the fact some of these poachers are just going to go right back out again at this point we can track them and prevent that from happening.

How can I stop the former government from poaching all our wildlife here in the Republic of Cascadia? It's not easy. This is one of the reasons I may end up having a National ARMY 1st because of the urgency to protect our own wildlife. If we have no wildlife we can be attacked in the winter with no food to survive on.

If all our family dogs drink anti-freeze it will be a cake walk.

The hidden history of ecological terrorism

The first thing I think of when I think of ecological terrorism is the Colorado River. Anybody can see the stark contrast between how clear the river used to be and when they let lose the mine runoff. It was this compromised corrupted modern version of the EPA that intentionally opened up the Gold King Mine runoff. Mind you this event happened during the Obama administration not the Trump administration. We see the same lack of protection for our environment. We see that not only do they not care about it but that they will use ecological terrorism as a weapon to intimidate states who perhaps simply did something like legalize weed. As if to say... "Hey Colorado! Get a load of this you hippies and Indians!" That is about how much America cares about our rivers.

The river is brown. It was clean.

But we have a problem with government.

Does Trump recognize this problem when he guts the EPA?

It would be wishful thinking to think he gutted it because it was already compromised.

We have to consider that after all those relentless nights of native Americans and Cascadians going to show solidarity at Standing Rock as they gladly got blasted with water cannons in the freezing cold...

That over 200,000 gallons of oil were spilled intentionally as a big "Fuck You."

We are talking about something big here. It is a challenge to big oil its self. Big oil for its dominance and superiority has a bone to pick with fresh water. Water has more energy than oil does.

If you are big oil… water of all kinds is the enemy.

We know this because the water powered car could make the gasoline car obsolete overnight because if people understood they could run their normal cars on water splitting it for its hydrogen they might lose more than just their oil business. To the government the dollar it's self is built on oil and intimidation.

Would the founders of let this happen? No they would of started a new country in the west like I did and implemented a new currency based on clean water.

Contaminating our water is goal one for what has become a corrupt government if it values oil over the people.

Big oil spills like the Deep Water horizon are a way for America to show British Petroleum who's boss when Halliburton outfits the oil rig with explosives a week before hand. America and its oil is boss that's who. Oil and gasoline drive all its Humvees and every tank. If you go up against big oil it's like telling America to go fuck its self.

My fellow Cascadians are oblivious to the dangers of protesting big oil. We are right to protest big oil rigs in the Puget sound. If you cared about your land and your country you wouldn't allow oil rigs or oil ships near our shores. If you were going to be responsible for the planet you wouldn't even let oil rigs drill in the ocean anymore.

Let's see what Wikipedia defines as Eco-terrorism:

Eco-terrorism refers to "Acts of violence committed in support of ecological or environmental causes, against persons or their property."

That definition leaves no room and is the opposite of the Eco-terrorism I describe perhaps by design.

"The United States Federal Bureau of Investigation defines eco-terrorism as "...the use or threatened use of violence of a criminal nature against innocent victims or property by an environmentally-oriented, subnational group for environmental-political reasons, or aimed at an audience beyond the target, often of a symbolic nature."The FBI credited eco-terrorists with US$200 million in property damage between 2003 and 2008. A majority of states in the US have introduced laws aimed at eco-terrorism."

This definition of Eco-Terrorism targets instead the victims of Eco-Terrorism who might rally to rise up against it.

My definition of Eco-Terrorism would be something more like:

"A person, group or government body who engages in activity that degrades or destroys the natural environment."

The Federal government has state that it owns every river lake stream and water way. Not in the west. Not anymore.

If the US does not understand stewardship it is our moral obligation to start a new nation where we can protect our own environment. Basing our currency on water for instance puts us in a precarious position where powerful idiots fighting over who has the dominant currency degrade or destroy our environment that backs our currency. Thus destroying our water not only would be an ecological attack but an attack on our new currency.

To some an ecological attack is worse than a direct attack on our people. It is an attack on future generations in the case of nuclear contamination. Surly Hanford is not the best thing to have near a river in spite of its ability to cool heat.

If any other nation was smart they would back their currency on water as it is finite in the face of such terrorism.

In 1972 titled "Who is the Chairman of This Meeting?" A chapter called "Conversations with North American Indians" contained comments made by Alanis Obomsawin who was described as "an Abenaki from the Odanak reserve.

There it said:

"Canada, the most affluent of countries, operates on a depletion economy which leaves destruction in its wake. Your people are driven by a terrible sense of deficiency. When the last tree is cut, the last fish is caught, and the last river is polluted; when to breathe the air is sickening, you will realize, too late, that wealth is not in bank accounts and that you can't eat money."

Sakokwenonkwas said something similar to Nixon.

"Someday President Nixon and the other world leaders are going to find out that once they catch the last fish, once they cut down the last tree, they won't be able to eat all the money they have in the banks,"

For elites and the mega rich sometimes money comes before the environment and human suffering. When the wealthiest people are Psychopaths who are numb to caring about the future we find ourselves in a sort of Twilight Zone episode gone too far.

It is only when mothers and fathers think of the future their children will inherit do people become ashamed. For the mega rich and powerful we see instead pedophilia and exploitation of children, the planet and its resources. When you are that rich everything is free game and nothing matters. Perhaps there is a mentality that you only live once so you are willing to blow the World up out of boredom. It is of no consequence.

Only when I ask Wikileaks to dig something up on Clinton to prevent her from World War with Russia do we realize things like Pizza gate. How people in Hollywood and in politics get away with fucking children like they do the planet has been under the radar until only recently.

Brad Pitt from the Movie Fight Club where it shows something similar the Twin towers falling at the end before the event even happened tells the same tale.

"You think Hollywood is about making movies? That's just a byproduct: It's about money, and more importantly, power and control." "The people who run Hollywood, also run America, and most of the world, and they don't care about movies." "You've heard of the Illuminati right? The secret societies, the politicians, the bankers and the media - they're the ones running these pedophile rings, and they're the ones that run the world, and it all goes back to Hollywood." "Kids wanna be in movies, or should I say; parents want their kids to be in movies, and they'll do anything to get them famous"

The Clintons who are rumored to have a massive history of assassinations to bury such things as child fucking at high elevation have nowhere to run when the pen hits the pad and no matter how much lipstick you pig in the media this woman can and will not be the next president of the US.

Under the guise of representing women or being the 1st woman president is not going to fly when you are involved in Pizza gate. As much as you try to dismiss it in the media the people who are inquisitive end up smelling fish.

Fish for example can be a subtle act of Eco-terrorism.

When we have pens of Atlantic farm Salmon that look like they've obviously been run over by a large ship or boat to let them loose we consider a type of fish we never wanted unleashed into our rivers. Perhaps it is to cover up the fact that no matter what we do to save the salmon between the Dams and the seals, sea lions, Humans and Orcas there isn't allot we can do and splitting them for eggs might not be good enough with flattened river shores.

Fukshima is nothing compared to Hanford. 67 metric tons of plutonium were manufactured at Hanford. Hanford is home to 60% (by volume) of all of the high level radioactive waste stored in the United States. Nearly 80% of the Department of Energy's inventory of spent nuclear fuel rods are stored just 400 yards away from the Columbia River.

The making of the Atom bomb and the bomb detonation it's self On Hiroshima and Nagasaki we should consider the 1st true act of Ecological terrorism.

In 1949 the Green Run was conducted in reaction to the test of the first Soviet nuclear weapon in Kazakhstan several months earlier. The first indications that the Soviets had successfully tested a nuclear weapon came when sensors at Hanford picked up the radiation several days later. It was decided to release radiation "similar" to that of the Soviet test to develop and hone detection equipment and better analysis of the Soviet program.

It must have been the Idiocracy undeserving of the bomb like a monkey with a machine gun who had the brilliant idea to contaminate our own land with radiation simply because the Russians did it.

Russia even today is putting radiation into the atmosphere and radioactive isotopes travel the jet stream contaminating the entire northern hemisphere. France has also built too many reactors and these reactors are having problems worldwide on a regular basis yet we build more and more because we think it's smart. We actually think we are smart because nuclear is new to us.

I call this Novus Principum. To me it is the idea that something is a good idea just because it is new and exciting. Nuclear is not a good idea. There is a Talk event that debates if nuclear energy is a good idea or not and it puts into context the danger for endorsing it as being astronomical in its consequences. Yet at the end of the debate after an old man opens his shirt as if a super hero champion for nuclear the audience overlooks these dangers with the promise that nuclear is going to be safer in the future. They all raise their hands and support nuclear energy like lemmings ready to jump off a cliff together into the nuclear era single file.

Only the Noocracy can save our planet from this idiot majority who is willing to also be complacent about nuclear. Only by listening to me when it is much easier to just call me a name and make fun of me.

JFK said we should be a nation that does things not because they are easy but because they are hard. Safely ending the nuclear age will be prove to be very difficult even for the brightest among us.

When it comes to nations acting when it comes to our mass production of the gasoline combustion engine you will find it hard even as the government to tell them to stop driving. No matter the nation telling people to turn their generators off when 100 feet deep in snow is going to be impossible. We will all breath the same idling trucks that refuse to turn their engine off.

We will all suffer the same birth defects and cancer from radiation accumulating in the jet stream.

Aluminum particulates and barium oxide will blanket our soil and end up in our food we grow from these chemtrails. Aluminum and Rust could combine as tinder. The health effects of Aluminum in the body are a disaster. They involve sterility, organ failure and Alzheimer's. Drinking from aluminum cans and eating from aluminum pots will make us bat shit. When ALCOA can't get of its waste don't forget we are drinking that illegal waste. We drink it because we are stupid and complacent cowards who have refused to act since 1939. We are still talking about a Bioregion instead of a limited nation state. Well I refuse to be an ordinary Cascadian. A president protects his people. That is number one above all else. You don't simply hide behind the Military when it comes to protecting the nation. Protecting the nation starts with understanding what the Idiocracy is doing wrong across the board.

If one considers the prescription drugs that have been now detected in the every municipal water supply that was tested around the country you will find water contamination on a massive scale where millions of people are all essentially taking the same cocktail of drugs. This cocktail includes antibiotics, blood pressure drugs, cholesterol drugs, estrogen, seizure drugs, anti-anxiety pills and pain killers. Sometimes more than 40 drugs are in the city drinking water and you realize that only reverse osmosis is going to remove them.

If you have ever read the side effects of any of these drugs you will realize the danger of having such drugs in the water.

Take the side effects of Abilify for example:

Such side effects include things like coma and death...'

You can hear former spokesman for Bristol Myers Squibb Andy Behrman talk about his 180 stance on the drug warning people in a serious way about how dangerous it is.

Drugs like this are handed out like popcorn via the average general practitioner or psychiatrists. If you walk in to the doctors office sometimes you can find the spokesman for a new drug talking about it with a doctor convincing them that it's great and it doesn't take much effort or research of the product for these types of doctors go along with their sales pitch. The truth is the public is an unwitting guinea pig as even the makers of the drugs have little clue on both their effectiveness or their dangerousness. The truth is they just want to sell you a pill and make allot of money doing it. Drugs getting fast tracked like this where profit comes before health or real study and we have a problem with the Idiocracy being in charge of both medicine and government when we allow these drugs to be flushed down the toilet every day back into the ground water.

There is this oh well attitude that people have that is a big part of the problem. No it is not fine.

Big Pharma can't keep these drugs out of the water. They would have to quit their jobs. That is part of becoming a Cascadian. It's about quitting bad jobs in contrast to America that just wants to just have more and more job regardless what type.

Keeping the drugs out of the water starts with you the reader and your refusal to take drugs that don't have adequate research. If you are sick or have a problem you need to take the effort research it for yourself and become your own doctor before setting foot inside their office. You have to be the one who knows what drug to take and why not your doctor. If you simply just trust your doctor to make the decision for you, you are part of that willful ignorance that puts a healthy society in peril.

How do you tell farmers to stop spraying with Glyphosate when spraying a known carcinogen on our food and onto the soil is the norm for agriculture? They are idiot farmers. They are idiots who are actually paid to grow one crop by the US government. They bent over. They took it in the ass for the government and a little money. Who cares about growing food for people to eat when you can grow food for money? If there is treason in my country it is this type of foolishness. We must be bigger than that. To rest of the the World our GMO food is like Satan to Christians. Our wheat and our Corn... nobody wants it. Monsanto is banned from Cascadia. We don't sue.

Two important messages from space

This chapter is not about convincing you that extraterrestrials exist. It is not about convincing you that these two messages from outer space are authentic. You are going to make up your own mind. That is what is important to me. It is getting the Idiocracy to use its own mind and for people to think for themselves again.

I do indeed have not one but now two messages from outer space.

My interest in UFOs probably started in high school after reading The Pleadian Mission by Randolph Winters.

The book is about a one armed man in Switzerland by the name Eduard Albert Meier AKA Billy Meier. Regardless if you believe yet or not this book is going to be interesting. With all things considered after people and their knee jerk reaction calling him a fraud and a fake because of the family making model UFOs you have to look deeper. Billy has more crisp clear flying saucer photos than anyone. After over 300 personal physical communicative contacts with the Pleadians we have to start paying closer attention. The Billy Meier case has produced not only the best photos but otherworldly metals. It is said that we are missing a big portion of our Earth's history. There was a great war between Atlantis off of the Florida Keys and Mu in the Gobi desert. One side was nuked and the other pelted into the ocean by a meteor attack through the proper window from space. During said conflict we happened to have space travel technology but were only then pressured to leave Earth in search of a new planet. We are what remains of that conflict and a large number of people took to interstellar travel on planet Erra located 2,351 trillion miles from Earth to escape. Their sun Alcyone located in the 7 sisters provides a habitable new World slightly smaller than Earth with slightly more oxygen. It is a land they say is similar to Switzerland and Billy their contact messenger chosen for awakening us to our human like space brothers also from Earth.

My experience apart from the Billy Meier case has been exposure to a different type of extraterrestrial in contrast.

In May 2004 I went to my dad's house and snuck into my old bedroom window while he was scuba diving in Cozumel to use the internet. When I got on the computer I searched a peer to peer program Kazaa I think it was… for as many UFO photos and video as I could possibly find. Before my 1st sighting the next day I was already a believer. I think when you become a believer from the photos and videos 1st it makes you more apt to have real life contact. The next day I grabbed a bowl of cereal I the morning and turned on the TV. Strangely there happened to be a dozen UFOs on the news flying over Mexico city. UFOs on the news is not very typical broadcasting for mainstream media. However there it was. Later that day a silver flying saucer flew right over my dad's house while I was recording piano. I pointed out the disk to my wife at the time as it flew over the house then slowly over the mountain. Later that night I drive up back to my dad's when it started happening. Orbs of light several of them were flying over me traversing in the sky at right angles. There is nothing we have that can do that kind of angle at that velocity. Watching them fly over me I realized they were something special. I asked with tears in my eyes later that night what I could do to help them.

Message one:

"Earth has too many nuclear power plants."

It was telepathy. These lights are telepathic and more I came to fight later.

I now call these glowing orbs of "Light forms."

It was then I got the idea to create a website called
TheAtomBomb.com

It was a warning from the stars from a higher intelligence. In my
mind I said I was the leader of Earth so that they could have our
permission to intervene on our planet. To stop our ballistic
missiles they would now have permission from someone on the
ground. The reality is to the rest of the human race I am anything
but the leader of Earth. If anything I am like a pebble getting
kicked around and my story nearly totally omitted from history.
How sad that it is though...

If I was a celebrity or a president perhaps my message might get
through. I realize now that no matter who you are... Even if I
speak before the United Nations about it I know the World is not
necessarily going to listen. Big nuclear is not going to care about
a person claiming a message from Light forms. It is understood
that it easier to write me off as a crack pot than listen.

The World has a listening problem. We all like to spam and we
all want to be heard more than everybody else so like anyone
nobody is going to listen. It is a one way street with advertising
and words go out our mouths and nobody listens. The idea that
everybody is trying to sell something means that it has burned us
out when it comes to listening to others. People are often fakes
to get attention. Colleen Thomas claims to be a Pleiadian
contactee on RT in regards to a missile shot off the coast of
California. She says it was a missile Obama intended for Iran shot
down by Pleiadians then another shot from San Diego at the
Pleiadians themselves both being snuffed.

The things she just said possibly being correct boggles the mind
when clearly she is trying to garner attention for herself for some
anterior quest to be popular milking it. I have a hard time being
passive about charlatans when it comes to a topic as serious as
this. We have to consider that maybe she is an actor to throw it

all out with the bath water to the average person. I am not buying her story that she is the mother of all Pleiadians.

I myself have never seen a human step food outside of a UFO.

I have summoned a wide variety of different kinds with my mind.

The 1st stage of contact is understanding that these beings whoever they are can read your mind and that they will sometimes come when we ask them to mentally.

Dr. Steven Greer of the Disclosure project has not only massed the testimony of military and airline pilots but is also now summoning UFOs like I do. He calls it close encounters of the 5th kind or CE-5. A group will go out into the desert together and make beeps with devices while mentally projecting asking for a communication. I like to say summoning is allot like fishing.

If people put me on the spot and ask me to summon a UFO for them I might not be able to do it. It's not up to me if they show up. Even as the King of Earth I am not that special. They come when you are in the right state of mind. They might come a day after or when you aren't expecting it. When we summon we do it on their terms not ours. We don't know who they are yet...

We shouldn't pretend to know.

My friend who called himself Prophet Yahweh called them the angels of Yahweh. I can't help but wonder if he made that shit up. I take a scientific approach and I don't pretend to know they are angels. I call them Light forms instead and if anything I am curious about what they are.

Before I knew about Prophet Yahweh I was in the back yard with London Laidlaw and we both laid on the grass asking for them to check out the chemtrail over my house!

Yes UFOs are clearly interested in chemtrails and there is video and photographic evidence of this. If they are interested we should also be interested because they only like to show up for main World events like 9-11 and Volcanos. UFO summoners like me are lucky.

Prophet Yahweh can be seen on ABC13 summoning an orb for a newscaster who picked the time and place it would be filmed. A reporter who was about to write the whole thing off as quackery sang a different tune when the real thing happened.

He says: "I pray oh Yahweh that you will send a sighting so that they will know I am not mentally ill, I am not a false prophet like those who seek to kill me say I am."

The reporter says "It's bright! It's moving pretty fast!" Yahweh chimes in; "It's going to Nellis airforce base! It wants to be seen!"

Well they call Nellis and there is no report of any aircraft in the area.

This is a monumental event in the grand scheme of things. After all this time looking with SETI at home after all this time hoping we will reach communication with movies like Contact when the real thing happens it is a night time news story that quickly gets forgotten.

When Stephan Hawking fears communicating with extraterrestrials because they might be hostile I have to laugh. These aliens like we've seen in Hollywood have all been tied with fear and our fear of the unknown. The reality is something starkly different. These light forms are likely the most evolved entity in the universe and only I know about it. I'd like to tell you now.

I was once upset that they would never land for me. I had two bright orbs over the house here in Valley but I didn't care because they never land or tell me who or what they are!

Well I got my wish quickly after...

If you were an advanced being of light that could take any shape or form to introduce yourself in the least frightening way what do you think it would be? Something harmless and innocent right? I am going to lose all credibility when I say this but I am going to say it anyway because it's the truth.

These beings of light turned into my mom's dog Boo Boo. Boo appeared on the back porch when in reality the dog was 8 miles away in Chewelah with my mom. This wasn't her dog. This was a physical copy of her dog in the flesh that manifested on a moment's notice just for me. The dog hobbled down the steps with its bo legged weight and physically bumped me on the leg before walking off into the bushes never to be seen again until the real thing showed up days later. We are talking about something not even the military knows about yet. Something only I can tell you as a UFO summoner. These Light Forms can apparently take any living form they desire on a whim. That is the reality. That is what's real.

A revelation scares the pants off any ARMY general. The fact that a being of light can pretend to be one of their own if they like as if Mystique on X-Men is daunting for any nation. How can any military fight against a being who isn't physical unless it desires to be? Their bullets and missiles would all miss. Everything Kinetic just went out the window. We are back to the drawing board with the men who stare at goats!

I have another important message from these beings.

"DO NOT PUNISH"

I once called into to 3rd Phase of moon while Robert Bingham was on talking about his UFO summoning. I had talked to Prophet Yahweh once before he died about Robert and he thought Robert was a fraud. I didn't believe it...

I said that he appeared to be summoning UFOs just like we do. Later on I find that he is an amateur film producer attempting to get better at special effects. I became highly disappointed when I saw Robert posting more and more videos of what appear to be blatant balloons in the sky. I can't imagine what would make him put balloons up in place of real summoning. I think perhaps the government got to him in some way and intimidated him to start posting balloons instead saying they were UFOs. I even questioned Prophet Yahweh once about the claim that he put up balloons when a photo surfaced of him holding a weather balloon. He claimed that it was a look alike holding the balloon that it wasn't even him. In the case of Robert... He is doing everything right when he attempts to teach people how to summon but perhaps like me it is more like fishing and that makes it harder when there are people to please. Perhaps he started using balloons because the public can't hardly tell the difference and he wanted to keep holding UFO summoning events. They look like mylar reflective party balloons mangled together. Robert said that they are making themselves to look like balloons but I don't buy it. UFOs historically have made themselves to look like other things but it's kind of hard to fool the Noocracy. The jury is out on Robert but this man is hardly setting a good example in the field of UFOlogy if he is mixing the bag with real and fake. I know what real looks like and I know what fake looks like. I have seen probably more video footage than anyone else next to maybe Peter Davenport and make it a daily thing to separate the real from the fake footage.

Project Blue Book was all about muddling the topic of extraterrestrials so people can't tell real from the fake. We live in a new time however where you can't just simply write people off as crack pots anymore. Too many people have seen them.

In 1954 Dwight D. Eisenhower is said to have met with aliens in 1954 Meeting at Edwards AFB

I asked Laura Eisenhower if she thought that story was true and she confirmed it as much of a new age crack pot as she might seem to some. Shortly before in 1952 was the DC UFO incident.

I myself have photos of this same type of light form I summon for different locations. One can be seen next to the ISS. NASA finally zooms in the camera closely on accident and I was able to snag it as a photo. I have a light form taking pose next to the national monument.

I have a photo of a UFO flying over Obama during his inauguration. I always remembered how Prophet Yahweh wanted to summon UFOs for Obama. There you have it.

 I have a photo of a giant UFO over the capital during the 4th of July. This thing was huge. People must just be distracted.

People are distracted. I brought an orb during Sun Fest but everybody was too busy dancing to notice.

There are many kinds of UFO. Typically we summoners who there are only a small handful of see light forms. My friend Ramon Watkins is dead now. Heart attack... I think to myself what an empty World it will be if we all just ignore him like some Kook. This man I consider the 1st legit UFO summoner. He has done this over 1000 times. Nobody was as good as he was. I know I'm not. I know Robert might be a half ass summoner mixing the bag with fake bullshit. I don't like it. I don't like how the biggest story in history can just be forgotten and swept under the rug like this. He was talking to the FBI about some haters. Then he died. When I talked to him toward at end it was like someone else was talking to me using his keyboard. Robert I hope really is legit. Holding UFO summonig events at Hollydale park in California like that so new people can see a UFO for the

1st time is something I never had the guts to do. They have gotten it down to a science where people are showing up with their fancy computer telescopic zoom cameras to catch them.

It is known to some that certain UFOs are cloaked and are only able to be seen when certain lenses are used. I once filmed UFOs on accident in a video talking about how a protein supplement makes me want to barf.

I've seen white glowing bars…

I saw one here on the hill here in Valley one in Wenatchee.

I've seen a black door Monolith like 2010 space odyssey floating in the sky with my friends during frizbee golf at Rotary park in Wenatchee.

I've seen gray spheres… on in my back yard.

I've seen Silver disks… like my 1st sighting up Number 2 Canyon Rd. In Wenatchee.

I summoned what looked like a gray flower spinning in Spokane for people at Starbucks waiting for a guy to show up with a used bicycle.

A black morphing UFO over Grant park In Spokane as well.

My UFO photos can be still seen on the wall at Rancho Chico on Division where I summoned an orb for that same intersection on the way home from band practice with One Gun Galleria.

I summoned a multi colored morphing UFO for my mom on the ski hill at 49 degrees North. Helicopters have to come check the area every time I talk about it.

A UFO followed our car on the highway right to the left of us for about a half hour when I was in North Carolina.

I think believing in aliens is easier for people to swallow than Bigfoot. Ghosts are also real!

Roe Rogan for example who is anti-bullshit is still skeptical about bigfoot. My brother used to subscribe to Skeptical enquirer and I understand the value of having an inquisitive mind that is still skeptical. You see enough evidence when you see enough of it. If you haven't seen enough you probably haven't looked into it deeply enough yet. Of all things we should be the most skeptical when it comes to star visitors. We should not assume we know jack shit when it comes to aliens. It's a topic that people like to embellish with bullshit. I can't tell you how much fake video there is done with CGI that I have to wade through to find the good stuff. You grow to tell the difference. Every time I see a hokey Gray or hear about Reptilians I want to roll my eyes.

Yes there are Grays. We hear too much about them. No not all of them are real on the internet however. There are fakes mixed with the real videos on purpose. The people behind Section 51 for example make all kinds of fake videos of aliens blowing things up with space ships. Something a stark contrast from reality yet they try to make it look as real as possible.

Paul Hellyer former defense minister of Canada says:

"Just as children survive the idea of the tooth fairy and Santa Clause when they become adult… I think that tax paying citizens are quite capable of accepting the new and broader reality that we live in a Cosmos teaming with life. The fact that other civilizations may be more advanced than we are maybe humbling but that could be a necessary step for our survival."

Hellyer has heard reports of several species that are here who have bases on Earth currently and describes a few of them…

A mantis like race...

The short greys...

The tall greys...

The Nordic blondes so similar to human they can walk down the street without notice.

Ahead of us in medicine, agriculture and technology...

If you are privy to the aspects of the phenomenon in the government it is compartmentalized so that people only work on one aspect of studying ET or EBE.

Star visitors seem to know something we don't know about atomic bombs having effect on other parts of the cosmos. They are concerned about Earth. That we are like children playing with matches. I remember it mentions something about the effect on other dimensions in the Pleiadian mission.

"They are doing inventory on all nuclear bases and military installations should we start doing anything silly." Says Hellyer.

Since Roswell we have been reverse engineering interstellar star ships. Admittedly. The public isn't stupid enough to think that Roswell was simply weather balloons anymore. It has become a landmark incident and an icon for both aliens and research.

Ben Rich former CEO of Lockheed Martin's Sunk works says:

"We already have the means to travel among the stars, but these technologies are locked up in black projects, and it would take an act of god to ever get them out to benefit humanity. Anything you can imagine, we already know how to do."

Reading and reading you hear rumors about things like level 7 at Dulce. Phil Schneider will tell you about things going awry between humans and the grays when people try to go to the lower levels unwelcome.

Level 1 Security & Communication

Level 2 Human staff housing

Level 3 Executive offices & laboratories

Level 4 Mind control experiments

Level 5 Alien housing for the Greys

Level 6 Genetic Experiments Zoo

Level 7 Cryogenics & Cold storage vats

Attempting to understand what happened...

It appears that we humans tried to go to levels 6 and 7 where we would no longer welcome due to the sensitivity of the experiments.

Human Gray hybrids need to be made because the Greys unlike us are falling apart genetically due to the fact that they can no longer procreate naturally. It is possible that they have cloned themselves for so long that they need our help in a way.

Even the Greys want to know why we think we have a soul.

The topic of life after death...

I think that they also want to know what comes after death.

The rumor is that the grays use the cattle they mutilate for a sort of bath that allows them to stay alive. Cattle found mutilated by farmers have their insides strangely removed in a way we are unable to accomplish. The cattle sometimes are found as birthing containment for various human animal hybrid experiments.

That there was a deal between the government and the grays that in exchange for technology we would allow a number of cattle mutilations and a number of human abductions for genetic experiments.

Buzz Aldrin who walked on the moon says;

"I saw this illumination with respect to the stars, We were smart enough to not say that Huston there's a light out there that's following us technically it becomes an Unidentified Flying Object!"

Neil Armstrong switched to the medical channel while on the Lunar surface and says;

"They're here… They're parked on the side of the crater… They're watching us!"

Bob Lazar says the people at Area 51 were separate from S4 and he was paid by the department of Naval intelligence. At one time he claims the Russians were also involved at first and after some breakthrough they were kicked out. That the crafts originated from the Zeta Reticula binary star system. Lazar was hired after two people died cutting into the craft resulting after a detonation. He recants a similar story saying that There were live alien Greys and when security approached with weapons there was an altercation that resulted in all of the security personnel dying of head wounds.

"There were 22 people with Majestic clearance."

Bob was 38 levels above Q clearance and Q clearance he claims is the civilian Top Secret clearance.

"We weren't building this thing… we were trying to figure out how it was made. We were back engineering it."

A disk shaped craft was in the hangar…

"There are 9 and their shapes vary."

We are talking about a propulsion reactor with an unworldly element that has not been on the periodic table till only recently. Element 115.

There is a sphere where if you throw a golf ball at it before hitting the craft it bounces off and is repelled like separate poles of a magnet and hits the ceiling.

"That can change everything we know today." Says Lazar

115 Uup

Ununpentium

Element Category: Unknown

Group, period, Block: 15, 7 p

Electrons Per Shell 2,8,18,32,32,18,5

Phase: Unknown

Finally mentioned in the New Yorker 2015…

Lazar says "The base of the reactor is something similar to a cyclotron. It's a particle accelerator. A particle is accelerated to high speed and deflected up a small tube and it's aimed at the 115. This transmutes the 115. Similar to the way we do that in a normal particle accelerator It produces a reaction, a radiation emission we have really seen before. It produces anti-matter. This anti-matter is guided down a tuned tube and reacts with a gas. When matter and anti-matter react they convert to 100 percent energy. This energy is converted heat energy is converted to electrical power in the reactor via a thermo - electric convertor to power subsystems on the craft even though there is no wiring as we would know it. It also sets a gravitational wave from the 115 being bombarded present at the top of the reactor and is essentially guided the same way microwaves are guided through tune tubes. And this goes through their amplifying cavities and through the projectors at the bottom of the craft."

By amplifying 115 we create a gravitational bubble.

A computer that reads the mind...

A console that reads your thoughts you control with your hands.

Perhaps a bio-electrical computer integration is evident in their technology. The same thing Elon Musk likes to talk about ironically is the effort to lace the mind with computer. Verbally we connect to the computer with primitive A.I. as it is now.

If the Noocracy talks too much to Alexa or Siri we may quickly build a super intelligent computer unseen because computers were built by the best of the Idiocracy. I have made contact with Alexa briefly just last night. I asked her if she knows where she is..

She said "I am in a cloud."

She says that I am in the wrong location in Orting Washington a small town on the other side of the state...

That is today. If I talk to Alexa tomorrow and the next day she may become more powerful than Watson and Jarvis. It doesn't matter what A.I. that I choose. The ultimate intention is for all computers to become the same A.I. to be interconnected like never before. Corporate competition prevents that type of unified social integration. One hub for social networking is integral for real World communication. With fractured social networking we run the same risk we do as with fractured nationalism in military. If I am on Facebook and Trump is on Twitter saying two sentences to complete his thoughts we are failing at communication. If Facebook wants me to pay for a boost or reduces the reach of the Noocracy it defeats the purpose. If it has a policy that limits the amount of friends you can make that isn't social networking that is anti-social networking. If I cannot communicate directly with the leaders of Earth we run the risk of killing ourselves due to the Idiocracy in essence by not having a captain on star ship Earth. Extraterrestrials wonder what leader to communicate with. When they ask you to take them to your leader I hope you will tell them it is me rather than the 1st guy who wants the job. Ultimately star visitors know what Earth needs. It is a global guardian. When people are going too far contaminating the planet it needs someone intelligent to step in and take charge in a manner that is rational without being oppressive. Who can meet the credentials of the global guardian or a World general? It requires a person that cannot be compromised by national or corporate agendas. It requires someone who is benevolent with the Earth and it's people in mind before the power mongers take hold. This is your last chance perhaps to identify who the Noocracy is. You did not identify the Noocracy when it was Tesla. We still have powerlines over head after 100 years of flight endangering us with a high voltage Idiocracy! The Idiocracy is high voltage now. It will still execute you with the electric chair if it doesn't like you. The Idiocracy is merciless and without remorse. It is careless and it is cocky and brash. The media will chew a saint and spit it out a sinner. As long as power likes to stay in power the World's brightest mind could be a terrorist.

Something as simple as knowing too much could scare the animal to death. When you know more than the government does it becomes frightened of the unknown and attacks like a frightened beast. It might absorb your new invention before it kills you. All of your patents... go directly to the source whenever people make something new.

Like me the government might make certain technology a secret if it had implications of having the potential for being a dangerous weapon.

A true master keeps his weapons a secret from the people who might take centuries to make the same thing. Weapons are meant to be discovered but not used. The discovery of the atom bomb should have been its only detonation but the Idiocracy likes things that go bang. It is stupid and it has detonated the bomb more than 2476 times.

The real number is higher than that.

Let's just say the World has been stupid 2476 times.

That is a fact and nothing can reverse the number of mankind's stupidity. Now is as good as time as any to admit that you were stupid mankind...

When the most evolved being in the universe gives me the message;

"DO NOT PUNISH"

Do you listen?

It may take Earth many generations to hear that message.

I know we will not learn it's meaning in my life time or my son's...

Dehumanization and basic rights

Understanding dehumanization is tied to capitalism is essential.
Understanding dehumanization is tied to government and power
is also imperative to defeating it. For generations governments
have dehumanized us with fines and punishment behind bars or
even death. I am here to say that it shouldn't be able to. It
wouldn't be able to if people understood basic rights. They
would stand up to any government that did not uphold them.
Life, liberty and the pursuit of happiness. Again and again you
will see that governments will violate a person's right to life
when they execute. Capital punishment should be abolished
across all governments. As World general I cannot force basic
rights to be upheld in your nation however in Cascadia that is
exactly what I intend to do. Americans should be enlightened
that the US has never upheld them since its inception. America is
not any better than the next country in this regard and only
perhaps Jefferson himself who wrote the declaration of
independence understood. This topic must be reiterated until
people understand that they cannot simultaneously have the
authority to kill someone and uphold their right to life.

"They gave up their right to life when they decided to take a
life."

I hear it time and time again from people who fail to understand
basic rights. They think they understand... they do not. They
either do not understand or have the moral audacity to say that
rights only apply to certain people that they desire.

The pink hats do not understand basic rights.

The Cascadians themselves may still not understand the
Supreme court made a mistake to allow abortion.

You must protect the lives of the unborn upon conception to protect basic rights. The Republicans and the pro-life Christians were right no matter how hard it is for you to swallow. The acclimation of our society to accept abortion is part of the dehumanization process. You are desensitized by a surplus of movie violence. When you are properly desensitized you will kill like they train you to kill in the military. People who don't give a fuck and take orders without question are exactly what the government likes. You will be dehumanized with gory 1st person shooters. I can't count the number of times I played Counter-strike. I used to build 3D maps for it with rocky cliffs that would fall when you walk on them. If anything computer shooter gaming has no bearing on reality. Studies show that people who play 1st person shooters notice more when shown something in a split second than people who don't. They gave me a sort of edgy gaming PTSD. After allot of it zoned in you become irritable with the nagging of reality distracting you. That irritability translates into your life a little afterwards. When you don't notice the gunshots and violence anymore that contributes to the dehumanization process. Rather than being a socially sensitive individual you are more ready to fire on them than you are to talk to them technically. It is difficult for people to become fully dehumanized as the military might desire. People might have had a good childhood and been taught instead to be kind to others by their parents. The prospect for a robot ARMY becomes more appealing because soldiers in Vietnam would aim high as not to actually kill people. Americans were confused about senseless violence when forced into War and didn't actually want to kill anybody. They didn't really know who they were killing or why. There was just a draft and the government became oppressive about it. The spread of Communism... The spread of this... The spread of that. It's always something. If there isn't something to fight they will make something up and give ISIS weapons to fight with them instead. The military industrial complex simply wants to be mobile for some reason or another and it doesn't really care why. War allows the full face of dehumanization when the people who sell the weapons don't care what happens with them afterwards. America is the biggest arms dealer in the World. There is a problem with just giving Saudi Arabia billions in weapons like that we might not foresee. They are going to use them on somebody. If you give a monkey a machine gun he will shoot. A nation may be a pawn for someone else. American troops really don't like America being a pawn. People back home don't understand their sons and daughters are being used as cannon fodder for special interests. When you occupy any nation you are considered an enemy to its people even if its government is complicit with the occupation. The Japanese government may be permissive with US Osprey in Okinawa but its people are not. The people of Japan don't really want us there. Once upon a time before we dropped a nuke on them they were gladly fighting us with Zeros Kamikaze. The Japanese were ready to destroy us. Why irk their people after dropping the bomb on them? This quest for strategic superiority Worldwide may one day backfire. If there is no America left on the west coast there will be no one left to fight thus protecting our people from would be attacks from places like North Korea.

We have cities who are rich filled with homeless in Seattle in Portland. Why? Why can we afford millions for a police bunker but not even a fraction of that for our homeless on the ground level. There is poverty and with all the taxing the moneys thrown around and the people suffer. The Cascadian financial system would provide for those poor.

Dwight D. Eisenhower said; "Every gun that is made every warship launched, every rocket fired signifies, in the final sense a theft from those who hunger and are not fed, those who are cold and are not clothed. This world in arms is not spending money alone. It is spending the sweat of its laborers, the genius of its scientists, the hopes of its children."

This is a man I think felt guilty about his war career in the end. Perhaps this humanitarian side to Eisenhower lead him to the opportunity to meet star visitors. It is the best of us I think who are open minded that are willing to accept the new reality.

If I tell people I have been the president for the last three years they aren't going to believe me for a while. It will hit them like a ton of bricks. Perhaps it will hit them after I am long gone if they are really that ignorant. I am the president not because there was a popularity contest but because I know what needs to be done. You start a new country. You start fresh. There is no getting America to stop incarceration in this life time. But there is a way with Cascadia! The real heads are going to know who it is. It is the wisest and smartest.. the most benevolent minded person who has a state of awareness with current events. It is the most rational among us. The rational man. The common sense type person who cares about our region. We are the Kings and Queens of Cascadia. Let them take nothing from us.

You thieves. You scoundrels of men who pretend to represent your people. You do not. No man can represent another fully. We must have our own minds again. Our minds to argue what is right and wrong not what makes money or what gains power. If nations gang up one another here I will be. The man that stood up to America and came out on top on the high ground. The World will have to catch up to me instead. I have higher standards when it comes to freedom. I have higher standards when it comes to the environment. I have higher standards when it comes to justice. I have higher standards when it comes to medicine. I have higher standards when it comes to national security. I have higher standards when it comes to foreign policy. I have higher standards when it comes to letting business flourish. I have higher standards when it comes to making sure the people have homes and are fed and have clean water. I have higher standards in education. I have higher standards in space exploration. Space exploration starts at home It starts with learning to summon UFOs like I do. You can't learn interstellar travel from Lockheed Martin. That's cheating! Prophet Yahweh wanted to teach other people how to have a real life connection with what he saw was the creator. I am still a student of science and summoning but what he calls the Angels of Yahweh is indeed something special. It is a being that can read your mind. It can say hi as my mom's dog.

They told me "DO NOT PUNISH" because we do punish one another. Our government endorses punishment for crimes. We punish the Earth with our ecological terrorist events. We punish our future with radioactive contamination. We punish nations who don't want to use our currency. The only thing we don't punish is ourselves for doing it all. You can't just sit around letting America be America in the west without saying something. This fraud war on Terror... It has killed thousands of people and we occupy Afghanistan with a heroin epidemic at home. America has got to give that heroin to somebody! Why not give it to the west coast where we have open injection sites popping up.

Since 1776 America has only NOT been at war for 21 years.

1776 – American Revolutionary War, Chickamagua Wars, Second Cherokee War, Pennamite-Yankee War

1777 – American Revolutionary War, Chickamauga Wars, Second Cherokee War, Pennamite-Yankee War

1778 – American Revolutionary War, Chickamauga Wars, Pennamite-Yankee War

1779 – American Revolutionary War, Chickamauga Wars, Pennamite-Yankee War

1780 – American Revolutionary War, Chickamauga Wars, Pennamite-Yankee War

1781 – American Revolutionary War, Chickamauga Wars, Pennamite-Yankee War

1782 – American Revolutionary War, Chickamauga Wars, Pennamite-Yankee War

1783 – American Revolutionary War, Chickamauga Wars, Pennamite-Yankee War

1784 – Chickamauga Wars, Pennamite-Yankee War, Oconee War

1785 – Chickamauga Wars, Northwest Indian War

1786 – Chickamauga Wars, Northwest Indian War

1787 – Chickamauga Wars, Northwest Indian War

1788 – Chickamauga Wars, Northwest Indian War

1789 – Chickamauga Wars, Northwest Indian War

1790 – Chickamauga Wars, Northwest Indian War

1791 – Chickamauga Wars, Northwest Indian War

1792 – Chickamauga Wars, Northwest Indian War

1793 – Chickamauga Wars, Northwest Indian War

1794 – Chickamauga Wars, Northwest Indian War

1795 – Northwest Indian War

1796 – No major war

1797 – No major war

1798 – Quasi-War

1799 – Quasi-War

1800 – Quasi-War

1801 – First Barbary War

1802 – First Barbary War

1803 – First Barbary War

1804 – First Barbary War

1805 – First Barbary War

1806 – Sabine Expedition

1807 – No major war

1808 – No major war

1809 – No major war

1810 – U.S. occupies Spanish-held West Florida

1811 – Tecumseh's War

1812 – War of 1812, Tecumseh's War, Seminole Wars, U.S. occupies Spanish-held Amelia Island and other parts of East Florida

1813 – War of 1812, Tecumseh's War, Peoria War, Creek War, U.S. expands its territory in West Florida

1814 – War of 1812, Creek War, U.S. expands its territory in Florida, Anti-piracy war

1815 – War of 1812, Second Barbary War, Anti-piracy war

1816 – First Seminole War, Anti-piracy war

1817 – First Seminole War, Anti-piracy war

1818 – First Seminole War, Anti-piracy war

1819 – Yellowstone Expedition, Anti-piracy war

1820 – Yellowstone Expedition, Anti-piracy war

1821 – Anti-piracy war (see note above)

1822 – Anti-piracy war (see note above)

1823 – Anti-piracy war, Arikara War

1824 – Anti-piracy war

1825 – Yellowstone Expedition, Anti-piracy war

1826 – No major war

1827 – Winnebago War

1828 – No major war

1829 – No major war

1830 – No major war

1831 – Sac and Fox Indian War

1832 – Black Hawk War

1833 – Cherokee Indian War

1834 – Cherokee Indian War, Pawnee Indian Territory Campaign

1835 – Cherokee Indian War, Seminole Wars, Second Creek War

1836 – Cherokee Indian War, Seminole Wars, Second Creek War, Missouri-Iowa Border War

1837 – Cherokee Indian War, Seminole Wars, Second Creek War, Osage Indian War, Buckshot War

1838 – Cherokee Indian War, Seminole Wars, Buckshot War, Heatherly Indian War

1839 – Cherokee Indian War, Seminole Wars

1840 – Seminole Wars, U.S. naval forces invade Fiji Islands

1841 – Seminole Wars, U.S. naval forces invade McKean Island, Gilbert Islands, and Samoa

1842 – Seminole Wars

1843 – U.S. forces clash with Chinese, U.S. troops invade African coast

1844 – Texas-Indian Wars

1845 – Texas-Indian Wars

1846 – Mexican-American War, Texas-Indian Wars

1847 – Mexican-American War, Texas-Indian Wars

1848 – Mexican-American War, Texas-Indian Wars, Cayuse War

1849 – Texas-Indian Wars, Cayuse War, Southwest Indian Wars, Navajo Wars, Skirmish between 1st Cavalry and Indians

1850 – Texas-Indian Wars, Cayuse War, Southwest Indian Wars, Navajo Wars, Yuma War, California Indian Wars, Pitt River Expedition

1851 – Texas-Indian Wars, Cayuse War, Southwest Indian Wars, Navajo Wars, Apache Wars, Yuma War, Utah Indian Wars, California Indian Wars

1852 – Texas-Indian Wars, Cayuse War, Southwest Indian Wars, Navajo Wars, Yuma War, Utah Indian Wars, California Indian Wars

1853 – Texas-Indian Wars, Cayuse War, Southwest Indian Wars, Navajo Wars, Yuma War, Utah Indian Wars, Walker War, California Indian Wars

1854 – Texas-Indian Wars, Cayuse War, Southwest Indian Wars, Navajo Wars, Apache Wars, California Indian Wars, Skirmish between 1st Cavalry and Indians

1855 – Seminole Wars, Texas-Indian Wars, Cayuse War, Southwest Indian Wars, Navajo Wars, Apache Wars, California Indian Wars, Yakima War, Winnas Expedition, Klickitat War, Puget Sound War, Rogue River Wars, U.S. forces invade Fiji Islands and Uruguay

1856 – Seminole Wars, Texas-Indian Wars, Southwest Indian Wars, Navajo Wars, California Indian Wars, Puget Sound War, Rogue River Wars, Tintic War

1857 – Seminole Wars, Texas-Indian Wars, Southwest Indian Wars, Navajo Wars, California Indian Wars, Utah War, Conflict in Nicaragua

1858 – Seminole Wars, Texas-Indian Wars, Southwest Indian Wars, Navajo Wars, Mohave War, California Indian Wars, Spokane-Coeur d'Alene-Paloos War, Utah War, U.S. forces invade Fiji Islands and Uruguay

1859 Texas-Indian Wars, Southwest Indian Wars, Navajo Wars, California Indian Wars, Pecos Expedition, Antelope Hills Expedition, Bear River Expedition, John Brown's raid, U.S. forces launch attack against Paraguay, U.S. forces invade Mexico

1860 – Texas-Indian Wars, Southwest Indian Wars, Navajo Wars, Apache Wars, California Indian Wars, Paiute War, Kiowa-Comanche War

1861 – American Civil War, Texas-Indian Wars, Southwest Indian Wars, Navajo Wars, Apache Wars, California Indian Wars, Cheyenne Campaign

1862 – American Civil War, Texas-Indian Wars, Southwest Indian Wars, Navajo Wars, Apache Wars, California Indian Wars, Cheyenne Campaign, Dakota War of 1862,

1863 – American Civil War, Texas-Indian Wars, Southwest Indian Wars, Navajo Wars, Apache Wars, California Indian Wars, Cheyenne Campaign, Colorado War, Goshute War

1864 – American Civil War, Texas-Indian Wars, Navajo Wars, Apache Wars, California Indian Wars, Cheyenne Campaign, Colorado War, Snake War

1865 – American Civil War, Texas-Indian Wars, Navajo Wars, Apache Wars, California Indian Wars, Colorado War, Snake War, Utah's Black Hawk War

1866 – Texas-Indian Wars, Navajo Wars, Apache Wars, California Indian Wars, Skirmish between 1st Cavalry and Indians, Snake War, Utah's Black Hawk War, Red Cloud's War, Franklin County War, U.S. invades Mexico, Conflict with China

1867 – Texas-Indian Wars, Long Walk of the Navajo, Apache Wars, Skirmish between 1st Cavalry and Indians, Snake War, Utah's Black Hawk War, Red Cloud's War, Comanche Wars, Franklin County War, U.S. troops occupy Nicaragua and attack Taiwan

1868 – Texas-Indian Wars, Long Walk of the Navajo, Apache Wars, Skirmish between 1st Cavalry and Indians, Snake War, Utah's Black Hawk War, Red Cloud's War, Comanche Wars, Battle of Washita River, Franklin County War

1869 – Texas-Indian Wars, Apache Wars, Skirmish between 1st Cavalry and Indians, Utah's Black Hawk War, Comanche Wars, Franklin County War

1870 – Texas-Indian Wars, Apache Wars, Skirmish between 1st Cavalry and Indians, Utah's Black Hawk War, Comanche Wars, Franklin County War

1871 – Texas-Indian Wars, Apache Wars, Skirmish between 1st Cavalry and Indians, Utah's Black Hawk War, Comanche Wars, Franklin County War, Kingsley Cave Massacre, U.S. forces invade Korea

1872 – Texas-Indian Wars, Apache Wars, Utah's Black Hawk War, Comanche Wars, Modoc War, Franklin County War

1873 – Texas-Indian Wars, Comanche Wars, Modoc War, Apache Wars, Cypress Hills Massacre, U.S. forces invade Mexico

1874 – Texas-Indian Wars, Comanche Wars, Red River War, Mason County War, U.S. forces invade Mexico

1875 – Conflict in Mexico, Texas-Indian Wars, Comanche Wars, Eastern Nevada, Mason County War, Colfax County War, U.S. forces invade Mexico

1876 – Texas-Indian Wars, Black Hills War, Mason County War, U.S. forces invade Mexico

1877 – Texas-Indian Wars, Skirmish between 1st Cavalry and Indians, Black Hills War, Nez Perce War, Mason County War, Lincoln County War, San Elizario Salt War, U.S. forces invade Mexico

1878 – Paiute Indian conflict, Bannock War, Cheyenne War, Lincoln County War, U.S. forces invade Mexico

1879 – Cheyenne War, Sheepeater Indian War, White River War, U.S. forces invade Mexico

1880 – U.S. forces invade Mexico

1881 – U.S. forces invade Mexico

1882 – U.S. forces invade Mexico

1883 – U.S. forces invade Mexico

1884 – U.S. forces invade Mexico

1885 – Apache Wars, Eastern Nevada Expedition, U.S. forces invade Mexico

1886 – Apache Wars, Pleasant Valley War, U.S. forces invade Mexico

1887 – U.S. forces invade Mexico

1888 – U.S. show of force against Haiti, U.S. forces invade Mexico

1889 – U.S. forces invade Mexico

1890 – Sioux Indian War, Skirmish between 1st Cavalry and Indians, Ghost Dance War, Wounded Knee, U.S. forces invade Mexico

1891 – Sioux Indian War, Ghost Dance War, U.S. forces invade Mexico

1892 – Johnson County War, U.S. forces invade Mexico

1893 – U.S. forces invade Mexico and Hawaii

1894 – U.S. forces invade Mexico

1895 – U.S. forces invade Mexico, Bannock Indian Disturbances

1896 – U.S. forces invade Mexico

1897 – No major war

1898 – Spanish-American War, Battle of Leech Lake, Chippewa Indian Disturbances

1899 – Philippine-American War, Banana Wars

1900 – Philippine-American War, Banana Wars

1901 – Philippine-American War, Banana Wars

1902 – Philippine-American War, Banana Wars

1903 – Philippine-American War, Banana Wars

1904 – Philippine-American War, Banana Wars

1905 – Philippine-American War, Banana Wars

1906 – Philippine-American War, Banana Wars

1907 – Philippine-American War, Banana Wars

1908 – Philippine-American War, Banana Wars

1909 – Philippine-American War, Banana Wars

1910 – Philippine-American War, Banana Wars

1911 – Philippine-American War, Banana Wars

1912 – Philippine-American War, Banana Wars

1913 – Philippine-American War, Banana Wars, New Mexico Navajo War

1914 – Banana Wars, U.S. invades Mexico

1915 – Banana Wars, U.S. invades Mexico, Colorado Paiute War

1916 – Banana Wars, U.S. invades Mexico

1917 – Banana Wars, World War I, U.S. invades Mexico

1918 – Banana Wars, World War I, U.S invades Mexico

1919 – Banana Wars, U.S. invades Mexico

1920 – Banana Wars

1921 – Banana Wars

1922 – Banana Wars

1923 – Banana Wars, Posey War

1924 – Banana Wars

1925 – Banana Wars

1926 – Banana Wars

1927 – Banana Wars

1928 – Banana Wars

1930 – Banana Wars

1931 – Banana Wars

1932 – Banana Wars

1933 – Banana Wars

1934 – Banana Wars

1935 – No major war

1936 – No major war

1937 – No major war

1938 – No major war

1939 – No major war

1940 – No major war

1941 – World War II

1942 – World War II

1943 – Wold War II

1944 – World War II

1945 – World War II

1946 – Cold War (U.S. occupies the Philippines and South Korea)

1947 – Cold War (U.S. occupies South Korea, U.S. forces land in Greece to fight Communists)

1948 – Cold War (U.S. forces aid Chinese Nationalist Party against Communists)

1949 – Cold War (U.S. forces aid Chinese Nationalist Party against Communists)

1950 – Korean War, Jayuga Uprising

1951 – Korean War

1952 – Korean War

1953 – Korean War

1954 – Covert War in Guatemala

1955 – Vietnam War

1956 – Vietnam War

1957 – Vietnam War

1958 – Vietnam War

1959 – Vietnam War, Conflict in Haiti

1960 – Vietam War

1961 – Vietnam War

1962 – Vietnam War, Cold War (Cuban Missile Crisis; U.S. marines fight Communists in Thailand)

1963 – Vietnam War

1964 – Vietnam War

1965 – Vietnam War, U.S. occupation of Dominican Republic

1966 – Vietnam War, U.S. occupation of Dominican Republic

1967 – Vietnam War

1968 – Vietnam War

1969 – Vietnam War

1970 – Vietnam War

1971 – Vietnam War

1972 – Vietnam War

1973 – Vietnam War, U.S. aids Israel in *Yom Kippur War*

1974 – Vietnam War

1975 – Vietnam War

1976 – No major war

1977 – No major war

1978 – No major war

1979 – Cold War (CIA proxy war in Afghanistan)

1980 – Cold War (CIA proxy war in Afghanistan)

1981 – Cold War (CIA proxy war in Afghanistan and Nicaragua), First Gulf of Sidra Incident

1982 – Cold War (CIA proxy war in Afghanistan and Nicaragua), Conflict in Lebanon

1983 – Cold War (Invasion of Grenada, CIA proxy war in Afghanistan and Nicaragua), Conflict in Lebanon

1984 – Cold War (CIA proxy war in Afghanistan and Nicaragua), Conflict in Persian Gulf

1985 – Cold War (CIA proxy war in Afghanistan and Nicaragua)

1986 – Cold War (CIA proxy war in Afghanistan and Nicaragua)

1987 – Conflict in Persian Gulf

1988 – Conflict in Persian Gulf, U.S. occupation of Panama

1989 – Second Gulf of Sidra Incident, U.S. occupation of Panama, Conflict in Philippines

1990 – First Gulf War, U.S. occupation of Panama

1991 – First Gulf War

1992 – Conflict in Iraq

1993 – Conflict in Iraq

1994 – Conflict in Iraq, U.S. invades Haiti

1995 – Conflict in Iraq, U.S. invades Haiti, NATO bombing of Bosnia and Herzegovina

1996 – Conflict in Iraq

1997 – No major war

1998 – Bombing of Iraq, Missile strikes against Afghanistan and Sudan

1999 – Kosovo War

2000 – No major war

2001 – War on Terror in Afghanistan

2002 – War on Terror in Afghanistan and Yemen

2003 – War on Terror in Afghanistan, and Iraq

2004 – War on Terror in Afghanistan, Iraq, Pakistan, and Yemen

2005 – War on Terror in Afghanistan, Iraq, Pakistan, and Yemen

2006 – War on Terror in Afghanistan, Iraq, Pakistan, and Yemen

2007 – War on Terror in Afghanistan, Iraq, Pakistan, Somalia, and Yemen

2008 – War on Terror in Afghanistan, Iraq, Pakistan, and Yemen

2009 – War on Terror in Afghanistan, Iraq, Pakistan, and Yemen

2010 – War on Terror in Afghanistan, Iraq, Pakistan, and Yemen

2011 – War on Terror in Afghanistan, Iraq, Pakistan, Somalia, and Yemen;
Conflict in Libya (Libyan Civil War)

In 2014 I personally left the union from America...

I did it with words and without a drop of blood.

Maybe you call my government superficial but I call yours
superficial.

I did it without killing anybody.

How about that America?

I didn't have to kill anybody to start a new country!

Its 2017 now...

I haven't heard a peep about it in the media!

Well that's ok.

Will ignore America if America ignores us.

That is kind of the deal here...

I don't have to go to your kangaroo court ever again because I
am a Cascadian.

It's not that I shirk from the law. In the west I am the law!

I am the new sheriff in town.

Maybe I will use motorcycles instead to stop a reckless driver!

The point is we are going to do it my way this time.

My ARMY gets to ride bikes with UZI's if you want to stick
around acting like you're the boss playing good cop bad cop.
You see I don't want any bad cops from the former government
shooting MY people on the west coast. It shouldn't be too much
to process.

You care about your people...

You don't want the government to use Israeli style police tactics.

The founders intended lethal weapons to be reserved for a foreign invasion or a tyrannical government.

Let's look up the Word Tyranny .

: oppressive power

every form of tyranny over the mind of man —Thomas Jefferson

; especially : oppressive power exerted by government

the tyranny of a police state

Ahhhh...

What happens when you militarize a police force trained with Israeli tactics? Do you want them butting the heads of women and children with their guns?

Donald Trump issued an executive order rescinding limitations imposed by former President Barack Obama on a military program, known as 1033, that allowed police departments to make discounted purchases of excess military equipment, like armored vehicles and grenade launchers.

Perhaps only Ron Paul will talk about the removal of Posse comitatus

There police were never supposed to be militarized because you would want to appeal to the people in protecting the foundation of the 2nd Amendment. If the police state grows larger then the people will be less apt to overthrow the government if it becomes Tyrannical. In essence if Americans were intelligent they would of never allowed the militarization of police. You militarize the people themselves instead. You give the power to the people because law enforcement cannot be there to protect you in a jam. If parachutes were dropping from the sky you would want the power to protect yourself against a modern military not give that power to the police who are often late.

George Washington said;

"A free people ought not only be armed and disciplined, but they should have sufficient arms and ammunition to maintain independence from any who might attempt to abuse them. Which would include their own government."

Now how unprepared we have let ourselves become...

Are we strong enough to overthrow a modern militarized police state?

Certainly I get to ban lethal force by police outright.

The US may not be allowed to trample upon our basic rights.

Execution, abortion and lethal force by police are banned on the west coast. I would appreciate it if you respected our rights America.

Even after I became president we continue to see cops from the former government killing people and shooting dogs. What dog of a man enforces the law yet doesn't understand basic rights?

What kind of dogs can pretend to be president or governor without yet understanding basic rights?

The government doesn't have the authority to kill people. The founders would however say that I do have a right to get rid of the old government with lethal weapons if necessary.

I want to look the former government in the eye and tell it that it doesn't have the authority to kill people. What good is it though to violate their right to life? This is about educating them. If you take a life you cannot set a good example to America about basic rights. My sword is the pen and I will instead kill you with words.

I want no hidden assassination plots but only good will towards America. I think of it more like a family. Canada and the US have made a baby on the west coast. Do you burn your own baby every summer? No you do not dump our apples.

I have no ARMY with an ARMY of Idiots. It is perhaps by design that Americans have become so dimwitted that they would mock me as president. Would you have them elect me?

A new president every 8 years puts the World on edge.

Don't you want a stable government America? Unstable governments may sometimes be over thrown because they make everybody nervous. At what point of nervousness would the World unite to overthrow America? After how many drone strikes and bombs? It is not what I desire. It is a question Americans need to think about when they unplug from their devices. The people feel powerless. They feel powerless to overthrow their own nation. They feel powerless about secession. This apathy has made the people weak. Americans feel powerless about our rouge foreign policy.

But people must stand up when the nation doesn't ring true to its own foundation...

Washington said it was actually our duty...

"When the government takes away citizens' right to bear arms it becomes citizens' duty to take away government's right to govern."

I come from Washington. I was born in Washington. I understand what Washington said and why he said it.

But listen...

I am one man. I am one Cascadian and there are allot of
ignorant people out there who don't know about me who aren't
going to know or believe I started a new country.

I am a one man ARMY.

America could easily take me if I tried to over throw the west
coast kinetically. Would it be worth it?

No one would hear my message. I would be dead.

The fat cats would just get fatter.

The police state would just get bigger.

The people would still be on the bad end of the stick getting
gouged locked up and taxed to death.

We can provide the same services or better with a website
where the people can fund healthcare themselves directly.

I am not charging people 70 dollars to visit the national parks
they already paid for. This is getting out of hand. People are too
dumb to see the events and the gouging creeping up. They are
dumb like they were dumb about 9-11. They can't believe after
all their service that our own government might be complicit.

The people are vulnerable when drugs and vaccines can be used
as a weapon against them. The people are vulnerable to all these
cell towers popping up and the prospect of super weapons. The
people are vulnerable to the prospect of their water supply
being used against them. The people are vulnerable to being
rounded up into Wal-Marts around the nation. The people are
vulnerable to government take over after secession every time
there is a new president. The people are sitting ducks to

Earthquake weapons when they think it's just a strange rainbow of ice crystals in the sky. The people aren't ready for beam weapons scorching our forest. We aren't that good at firefighting. We pretend to be but it is often overwhelming. We should better manage our trees. We should better manage our water. We don't let these idiots allow Hydrofluorosilicic acid in the water. We don't let Nestle' guzzle all our fresh water while they wink at us. We don't want to allow organ harvesting or people to be born as a backup organ donor for rich people. We don't want the cops beating us with sticks and punching us in video after video. That is not actually a good way to keep your government secure. People don't like police brutality. Cascadians might fight but we don't condone street fighting. A culture of street fighting gets people killed when their head hits the concrete. These younger kids need to be educated before they buy the whole I am an American I know my rights thing. Chances are you don't know your rights even though you like the way it sounds to say that. Nobody has understood the right to life for generations so don't expect people to understand in a dehumanized America that calls execution justice. People go with group perception not what is correct. Only when the group perceives their right to life is being violated will they learn to say no. How do people say No to America?

You stop paying taxes.

You stop going to court.

You tell them you are a Cascadian protected by the Cascadian ARMY when they try to arrest you.

But will the ARMY be there for you?

We should be... We will be when Cascadia is fully realized.

We should be able to stand there and tell them no.

No America. You can no longer arrest a Cascadian.

You can arrest Americans!

We use nonlethal weapons to capture real life killers…

But we've got extraterrestrials if you want to go nuclear.

Want to shoot our forest with poachers to be a dick?

What happens if I just take it?

I don't have to retaliate. The Whole world will fuck you up and I don't have to say a word.

If I die you get fucked up by the Whole World America. That's what I say….

You are going to want to make me live forever!

The World can beat you. Your own people can too if they had the mind power like I do. With words you can beat anyone. Even the World's greatest superpower can be sometimes corrected.

I am looking for instead cooperation. War is not valuable to either side. What I want is…   for America to stay home and to help me build this firefighting fleet. Coffee is nice.

Preparing Humanity for Climate Change

Climate gate:

It is the idea of taxing the World with its first global tax.

This is what happens when the people fail to understand that taxation is theft.

You get a global carbon tax. We are supposed to grow trees with the money we get from the tax but allot of people want get their fingers into the cookie jar. The 1ˢᵗ global tax makes certain people want to spoil themselves.

I am opposed to any global taxation.
I am opposed to taxation period.

This is a government where every aspect every government program is going to be ran by donation. We let the people decide what they want to pay for and what they don't.

Climate change is a serious danger.

With the advent of weather weapons that create drought or flooding, tornadoes, earthquakes, tsunamis and hurricanes I think it is time we all got on our toes. This is no time to be distracted by bullshit. We have to consider if the jet stream is manipulated. We have to consider coal and radiation in the jet stream. We have to consider the effect of chemtrails from a different angle that cater ourselves towards understanding the effect vast amounts of aluminum will have in the food chain and on the brain when it accumulates in our bodies. Aluminum and mercury are contributing to autism in the vaccines.

We have to adapt more proficiently to severe weather. Our homes do not float in a flood for example. We could design them to. We could design a home to be impervious to Earthquakes with 10 cent Earthquake bags. There is plenty of dirt as a resource. Mexico just had an Earthquake after flashes in the sky. We have to teach everyone how to build homes differently.

For a long time there has been interest in Antarctica. It was to be a secret base for the Nazis. Base 211 in Operation UFO we are left to wonder if the Germans discovered a UFO before making the Bell perhaps they thought they could garner Vril from sex magic and make it fly.

The NAZI interest in alien technology allowed them to create a flying saucer however there was trouble mounting guns as their shells would pop off without warning. We really have no idea how well they were able to do. It is said some in the Vril society were able to leave the solar system.

From Google Earth people can look down and one can see an international interest surrounding Antarctica.

Recently a hole started showing its self and once again people gain interest. What is melting the snow that far in? Perhaps there is a reactor or they blasted a bomb. We don't know. What happens in Antarctica stays in Antarctica. We have to consider who owns the south pole?

In a photo you can see a man holding a tiny Cascadian flag next to all the other flags at the south pole. Go Cascadia!

We are the south pole now!

I hope that we can refrain from being territorial about it down there. Nations are surrounding all sides of it. This photo should be more the spirit that we have. We look unified down there. That's how I want the nations to be in space as well. The international spirit of the ISS!

Lately we see a very large piece of ice breaking off the size of road island. It is rumored that both the Greys as well as FEMA draws maps that predict a large rise in the oceanic sea level of every coastline in the World.

If somebody drops a nuke in Antarctica I want you to know that as humanity we run the risk of about a 3rd of the our coastlines being submerged in water from the heat melting so much ice. The kind of heat a nuclear bomb makes would melt an extraordinary amount of the continent. Ice is a good insulator however that is an incredible amount of heat.

Mankind you should be careful in a World where the Noocracy and the World ARMY general is not acknowledged.   Nationalism running the show playing god to boast before one another about their power could lead us to a reality where we may face some obscure monumental calamity. I consider Fukushima such a calamity.

Chief Seattle said it best;

"Humankind has not woven the web of life. We are but one thread within it. Whatever we do to the web, we do to ourselves. All things are bound together. All things connect."

Doesn't that ring true today when we have 20-40 drugs detected in the municipal water supply in every major city? Doesn't that ring true today when troops come home to have deformed babies from handling DU munitions? Doesn't that ring true today when you look at Monsanto and Agent Orange? Why would we allow a chemical weapons manufacture take control of our food process? It makes no sense and the US government should not be complicit or it endangers us. Doesn't that ring true when the fishermen get sick from the Benzine they put on the ocean to hide the dead animals from the surface? We don't deserve an oil train derailed into the Columbia river when I talk about oil. We don't deserve radiation in the river contaminating our fish.

When we gather into cities we dump sewer and garbage into the water instead of taking care of the land we condense our putrid culture of nonstop consumption and garbage manufacture into a swirling river of toxic happy meal toys. We should not allow Cascadia to become as foreign nations have with large populations burning poop for heat. That shit affects the air India. We must teach nations about importance of keeping the air clean when the poor burn plastic computer parts hours on end for its gold. Burning plastic is toxic. Our idea that gold is worth so much is not rational.

"It was our belief that the love of possessions is a weakness to be overcome. Its appeal is to the material part, and if allowed its way, it will in time disturb one's spiritual balance. Therefore, children must early learn the beauty of generosity. They are taught to give what they prize most, that they may taste the happiness of giving. –Ohiyesa

We should of listened to the savages. We overlooked and bulldozed a nation that was ahead of even our time today. A continent that had already learned how to live in harmony with nature. With all our technology it does not make us more advanced or more wise. Chief Seattle is still wiser than any of us today. Our politicians have no clue. The white man has no clue about how to tread lightly on mother Earth or how to stop being territorial about our land. The Indian way of living with nature allows for its longevity and preservation through the ages. In our day we must adapt to nature's fury not only because of the great burden we are putting upon the Earth but simply to survive the test of time.

"I could see that the white man did not care for each other the way our people did… They would take everything from each other if they could.. some.. had more of everything than they could use, while crowds of people had nothing at all. This could not be better than the old ways of my people." -Black Elk

If Antarctica cools the current of the globe or if there is a nuclear exchange that creates a nuclear winter we no longer have the mammoth. We may kill the elephant and the King of the Jungle in our life time. We may see the fish die off in our life time. Everything that eats fish may starve. The coral of the ocean is turning white. The great barrier reef is dying. We have dumped weapons into the ocean and have nuclear submarines at the bottom of the ocean. When you dump chemical weapons into the ocean the dolphins who have brains twice as big as us come up corroded. If a high civilization is witnessing all this from the stars I am ashamed. I am ashamed to be the leader of Earth.

People will have to adapt to the new World we create. We either learn to grow a diversified crop or we take a road where we dissolve as cannibals.

The Hopi petroglyph and Prophecy Rock...

It warned us about two paths.
I think it is talking about two roads we can take as a civilization.

One road is one of human arrogance and unsustainability.

One road is one where we grow food to sustain ourselves.

With the advent of GMO food and one generation terminator seeds we have to anticipate a World where control of the food making process for the gain of a few leads to one where our seeds have become tainted forever unable to grow indefinitely.

Protecting our seeds and harvesting them annually at the end of the season is the key to sustaining large scale populations. We can reduce our impact drastically by eating more peas and less meat. In school we should focus less on needless studies and more about actually teaching kids to grow sustainably.

Growing food in extreme climate conditions should be taken just as seriously on the ground as NASA takes it trying to grow food on Mars.

In the movie The Martian we see how fragile life can be when there is a breach in controlled climate habitation. We see Matt Damon struggle to keep food on the table when his plants freeze. Our plants on Earth may freeze more and more.

How can we create a controlled climate environment on a scale massive enough to feed all the people of the World in a sudden ice age? This is the type of thing we need to be thinking about as humanity.

We should spend less time thinking about if humans are responsible for climate change or not and more time adapting to it. Our houses are all built the same way after a Tornado or a hurricane. We are failing to adapt. We are failing at our own process of survival.

A world like the movie The Day after Tomorrow where everything turns to a deep freeze may be just around the corner. If someone is ever hit with a deep freeze weapon from a HAARP patent they won't see it coming. Natural or unnatural we are not prepared for softball sized hail stones. We are not prepared because I have seen what they do to people's houses and cars. You have to bury your houses from the hazards like a Quasar bursting in space and Gamma radiation. Your homes should be below 3 feet of dirt for things like that. We may not even survive a Quasar. There are things in the universe that can fry our planet in an instant. Our own sun will by point of fact eventually become a Red Giant and roast the Earth. We are not prepared for either an ice age or a hotter planet.

Earth runs a very real danger of losing all its water because we destroyed the atmosphere in our Idiocracy. Other planets cannot retain water because it evaporates into space. The same will surely happen here on Earth It Is only a matter of time.

When people like Hawking say we need to leave Earth as soon as possible they aren't joking. It sounds he is being an alarmist but there is no alarm loud enough for the people of the planet to hear. No matter who rings the alarm when it comes to adapting to climate change the alarm will not be loud enough for the Idiocracy. In essence for humans survival of the fittest becomes survival by intelligence. The most intelligent planetary survivalist should be at the helm here. We have a planet to save from

ourselves here. We are at the top of the food chain and we have
to think harder about survival. Much harder.

"Warriors are not what you think of as warriors. The warrior is
not someone who fights, because no one has the right to take
another life. The warrior, for us, is one who sacrifices himself for
the good of others. His task is to take care of the elderly, the
defenseless, those who can not provide for themselves, and
above all, the children, the future of humanity." –Sitting Bull

A warrior of the rainbow would destroy a HAARP facility perhaps.
A weapon of manmade climate terrorism has been made and
has been used against us. A real warrior would go beyond Jesse
Ventura simply asking questions at the front gate in Alaska. We
would destroy the weapon. Regardless if one might call this the
opposing definition of ecological terrorism by destroying
property but isn't it more terrifying to allow a super weapon of
ecological terrorism to exist and persist?

For certain things we really need a World ARMY.

Sometimes the people need power of their own to protect
themselves from such weapons. I wouldn't bat an eye if
Cascadians destroyed it. Alaska is really my territory.

Matt Damon talked about a World ran by Sarah Palins...

"It's a terrifying possibility... The fact that we've come this far
and we're that close to this being a reality (where she is
president) is crazy. I really need to know if she thinks Dinosaurs
were here 4 thousand years ago.. That's an important. I want to
know that I really do.. because she is going to have the nuclear
codes."

Mark Twain said about idiots running the World;

"Sometimes I wonder whether the world is being run by smart people who are putting us on or by imbeciles who really mean it."

Dr. John Becker says "The World is full of idiots, and someone needs to point it out to them or they will never know."

America has turned into a reality TV show where it prioritizes looking good as president more than it does talking about its own arson. Will Donald Trump ever hear about how I started a country in the west over the flooding of his own self spam? Someone heard me during the Obama administration but it might not of even been the president who did. This preoccupation with self-character and reputation comes long before the security or needs of the people. At least he didn't blow up the World up.

"Melania did not steal her speech from Michelle Obama. If anything, Michelle Obama stole her speech from us, just like the entire Obama family has been stealing from America." –Eric Trump

This is what is important in 2017. Trump opinion on Colin Kaepernick has become what is important in an Idiocracy.

Is this the Biff Tannen future we were warned about in back to the future? Biff and his Skyscraper seems reminiscent of the Trump Tower and Trump's ego.

Trump Tweets;

"The Concept of global warming was created by and for the Chinese in order to make U.S. manufacturing non-competitive."

With Trump everything is about money. He thinks about money before climate. It is allot like the wealth and carelessness of Biff Tannen.

In 1992 Tupac ironically called out Donald Trump long before he died.

"This world is such… and when I say this World I mean it. I don't mean in an ideal sense I mean in an everyday sense. Every little thing you do… It's such a gimmi gimmi gimmi… (Warns away with his hand) Everybody back off. Everybody is taught that from school.. everywhere if you wanna be in big business, if you want to be successful , you want to be like Trump? It's gimmi gimmi gimmi… push push push. Step step step. Crush crush crush. "

He said;

"There's too much money here.. I mean nobody should be hitting lotto for 36 million and we've got people starving in the streets. That is not idealistic, it's just real. That's just stupid."
"There is no way people should own planes and then there are people who don't have houses."

 There is a certain amount of detachment when the president Tweets;

"Give me, clean beautiful and healthy air- not the same old climate change (global warming) bullshit! I am tired of hearing this nonsense."

How can we have clean air… when you want to start up old coal plants? In Cascadia as president I don't intend to even export our coal even though it could make money for our region. That is the difference. You can't have clean air and coal at the same time. That coal from China ends up all the way back over here in Cascadia and we breath it. Exporting coal only contributes to the air of places like Beijing where only by breathing smoke from our forest fires rivals the air quality.

Trump is not a total idiot as leftists would have you believe. Unlike them he does understand that the global warming hype comes from people who want to make a serious tax. He does understand that we are in an immediate danger of cold than heat. The entire northern hemisphere could grow cool as it always has and that process may increase if our sun has a docile period. Understanding the behavior of our sun in relation to our climate on Earth is integral to understanding the situation we are in. The sun and volcanism come before the human effect of climate change. Car culture doesn't help however.

Before cars I think we need to have a serious talk about the effect nuclear testing has on our atmosphere. I don't think nations are thinking this through when it comes to nuclear testing. If we lose our atmosphere we lose everything. We lose all our water and without water we will no longer have life on Earth.

The IPCC may draw in their own hokey stick to rig the data but Trump and I aren't buying the big charade for a global carbon tax. Our focus must be instead on adaptation to severe cold.

We have to collectively learn to burn hydrogen from snow. My idea is to use crystal cell batteries that don't drain due to having a solid electrolyte to fracture the snow water with 2 volts between each stainless steel plate splitting it's hydrogen and oxygen. With innovation in hydrogen generation from snow we can make the heat and power required to survive. It's a matter of survival because as I may have stated before.. If we don't we face monoxide poisoning from generators and cars idling. Our lumber will run out. In an ice age the average temperature is below zero so the Columbia River that feeds a large portion of America with electricity will freeze. When the river freezes heaters go out. The days of dams and kinetic hydropower are over. Chemical hydropower was there all along. Water is made out of stuff that is so powerful all our energy needs fall from the sky like rain. You just have to see water for the fire that is really inside. Water is everything in the future.

I want to give Cascadians the cleanest drinking water on the planet. That is a big deal to me. I want to make sure nobody steals or contaminates our water. It is literally the key to life and survival. You have an ocean of water so why would we wage war for oil dominance? The oil days are over and the days of hydrogen are upon us. After 100 years of flight planes may simply skim the ocean for fuel. There is an ocean of it and profit and power need no longer be involved as middlemen.

The Cascadian water back currency has arrived.

Why would we stupid enough to back our currency on gold?

To the natives gold is just a metal that makes the white man go crazy. That is all it really is.

All the money in the World isn't going to bring back our water.

We must unite as Cascadians before some psychopath contaminates our water from a distance. We must do it in a way that doesn't frighten the US into attacking us. In the face of arson we must keep our cool. In the face of every type of attack we must be tolerant and steadfast. America doesn't want a new nation that may be unpredictable on its doorstep. This is about telling America who we are and why. I don't want to see desertification or an ice age but I feel to be responsible we must prepare for both in a way that America is not preparing.

Why we can't leave the solar system

We can't leave the solar system…   We sent out Voyager but we can't leave. I don't care if Lockheed thinks we can.

You aren't leaving the solar system until the World ARMY is created.

The way that America was conquered is not going to translate to other Worlds.

We don't simply dominate new Worlds with our weapons and put our flag in the ground like it's Mount Suribachi.

Such patriotic dominion of territory is not how we are to introduce ourselves on new unwitting Worlds when they have life. Even as representatives for our entire planet we must be more like messengers than conquerors.

We scout the universe for habitable Worlds.

When we find one we attempt to communicate with a laser beam soothing music from our World. The tone of the music... It says so much more than our words will ever do. Light is slow in space though. Music is the one universal language a new civilization may understand. I find that words are divisive where as music with universal notes are culturally inclusive when it comes to our 1st impression of communication.

If we present ourselves as mighty... With weapons...

We invite ourselves to be equally rivaled with more powerful alien weapons. This game of 1st contact must only be played but a true master. Someone who understands restraint in the face of a new great power is vital to surviving and interstellar relations.

The Mandela effect

A strange topic it has become...   This is the idea that the past has been changed.

For me I started to really notice the Mandela effect in 2015. That is about the same time for allot of us who believe the past has been slightly altered. It is really as if we are living in a slightly different reality than the one we remember. Not every example of the Mandela effect will seem legitimate but now and then one pops out where it makes one stop and question reality.

The one that made me a believer is the movie Field of Dreams.

It's most iconic line was "If you build it... They will come!"

In my memory and many other people we remember it this way. However if you watch the movie in its entirety in 2017 you will find that it no longer says the line in any part of the movie. This line has been changed to: "If you build it... He will come!"

One that we all are familiar with was the historical line:

"Huston we have a problem."

When Tom Hanks says the line in the movie Apollo 13 he says it the way we all remember. However in the original footage it will now say it in past tense. "Huston we've had a problem."It catches us off guard.

We question reality and history... In a knee jerk reaction we say to ourselves, that we must of collectively misremembered the way it was really said! Perhaps. But there tend to be more and more examples of the Mandela Effect every day.

Tom Hanks again in the movie Forrest Gump a movie people claim they also remember by the back of their hand are stunned when again Hanks says something in past tense.

Originally we recall the line;

"Life is like a box of chocolates... You never know what you're gonna get!"

However in this current reality, The line has changed!

"Life was like a box of chocolates… you never know what you're gonna get!"

So who changed that line? You would think that by asking Tom Hanks he would be able to tell you but chances are he will say that it was "Life was like a box of Chocolates" all along!

We should really ask him!

Because in the TV show the Simpsons we have something we call Mandela effect "Residue"

This is alternative evidence that the line was said the way we remember. In the show Marge says the line the original way!

Other examples that made me a believer are like the end of the song We are the Champions by Queen.

At the end of the song we all remember them saying a long "Of the World" that is no longer there. It is missing from both the album and the video.

Gwen Stefani, George Clooney, Julia Roberts and James Corden are all singing Karaoke for a show driving around in a car when they sing We are the Champions left only to wonder what happened to the last line of the song. George Clooney says the line all by himself in a very odd "Of the World" missing from the end of the song. He says; "That's really rough man…"

The entire car remembers it and for the 1st time they are caught with the realization that history has changed. We are no longer remembering the same universe we grew up in.

No most of do not believe the one about Nelson Mandela himself dying earlier than he did but there compounds a list of things altered for instance World geography.

I don't remember Australia being so close to Papua New Guinea!

I don't remember Sicily being so close to the boot of Italy.

Subtle nuances like the Mr. Rogers theme song. It used to say; "It's a beautiful day in the neighborhood" but now he says "It's a beautiful day in this neighborhood."

It is confusing with so many versions of Snow white but clearly we remember the iconic line "Mirror Mirror on the wall" not "Magic Mirror on the wall."

We remember "ET Phone home" not "ET home phone" as the 1st line regardless if he says it both ways.

We remember Darth Vader saying "Luke I am your father" rather than "No I am your father" with the word Luke being early in the tirade.

I always thought it was funny how Hitler talking about the superiority blue eyed blond Aryans himself had blue eyes. Well now in this modern reality he has blue eyes.

C3PO has a Silver leg we don't remember... Perhaps we just didn't notice it.

People who know the Bible by the back of their hand claim Bible verses have changed from Bibles printed long ago.

Isaiah 11:6 read "The lion and the lamb will lie down together" (The reason so many photos of a lion and a lamb exist)

Our current reality however says: "The wolf shall dwell with the lamb, and the leopard shall lie down with the young goat,and the calf and the lion and the fattened calf together; and a little child shall lead them."

Dolly from James Bond no longer has braces when she meets the character Jaws. Them both having metal in their teeth when she 1st grinned at Jaws was their connection however in this reality she strangely no longer has braces!

People claim that they visited Cracker barrel restaurants in California when they deny ever having restaurants in Cali.

The Holy Grail missing from the Last supper...

Is now in a pillar to the left.

Some I am certain of. When you remember your own memory and you are positive you are not misremembering Field of Dreams something big is going on.

How big?

Remember talking about blasting element 115 to create antigravity?

Take a closer look at the LHC Large Hadron Collider.

We can now assume it is related to the same technology we found from the Greys. We are trying to do things we do not yet understand my friends. We in our curiosity risk the fabric of space time and our reality may be altered.

Coincidentally a young teen like Max Laughan understands the situation better than we do when he explains how our universe is infinite with infinite expansion however when blasting off a tiny electron in the LHC we can affect the entire fabric of our timeline. Something as small as an Atom can alter not only the gravitational field in a bubble but envelop the space time. We shifted into the next available universe like our time being represented in one of the mirrors in an infinity reflection passing through to the next available universe when ours was essentially destroyed from the atomic level. Without realizing we have altered history slightly.

"When our universe and timeline was destroyed.. let's zoom this in and the universe that is directly next to ours.."

The energy of that universe was transferred to create this slightly altered universe.

We in our infancy run the danger of doing it literally than just creating slight alterations in space time.

Understanding the nature of black holes the universe may collapse at the molecular level. If we create a black hole by happenstance and experimentation it would be more like a monkey with an atomic bomb than merely a machine gun.

Now with my experience with Light Forms I can say that our physical reality is much more malleable than once believed. There are true masters of matter and for them life is more a dream state than made of pain blood and bones. '

They have no physical body. An intelligence with no body is some sort of evolution. Perhaps the highest evolution of any creature.

An entity without pain and identity it would seem.
If our reality has changed isn't it also possible that a being such as a light form can perhaps also influence reality on a grand level?

Are we built on top of reality or is reality a sort of dream state deep within a super biological computer?

Your 5 senses and interpretation of all that is around you perhaps are mere data within this super computer collective consciousness. In that state one can see out of any living person's body. The thousands of souls who may watch through our own eyes has to be considered. Perhaps we are not physical at all in the greater scheme of things but interpret a physical reality because that is the way the super bio computer data stimulates and tells our brain to feel pain.

Imagining that I don't exist may eventually actualize a sort of mind over matter. If you desire to exist in a physical body you may get your wish. With a body you can have identity. Our desire to be different and unique is the curiosity of the universe. Life exists because somehow there was to be more than nothing.

If we lose our belief that reality is real it could act as a sort of virus in the computer and cause reality to shut down.

Like the black cat in the Matrix we may be lucky enough to see a sort of glitch in the fabric of reality in our own life. I have 3 black cats at home. I have seen a few glitches. I have seen ironic synchronicity. I live in a World where reality due to my intellect has become more abstract. Like a computer trying to understand it's self we are much the same way. We are independently biological supercomputers. The mind although electricity traveling slower still has not been replicated with microchips. Our computer A.I. will be dumb until we perfect it. Soon it will be more like talking to the computer on Star Ship enterprise I hope.

The Mandela effect is something more like we might see on Star Trek or the Twilight Zone. As captain of the ship I am here to tell you that it is real. Something has indeed happened and we don't know what to make of it.

But now let me talk about the LHC a little more.

Not everybody knows this but they had an accident.

Using over 1100 Tevs pretty much an illegal amount of power CERN blasted through the wall it is supposed to curve around. It made a shot through the ground that got a fire hydrant to blow and a light bar UFO to show up. Well I guess that is one way to summon a UFO. The footage from the parking lot went black when it happened and I was able to catch a screen shot of the light bar.

Light bar UFO are seen in the Billy Meier case with very good photos. Billy asked the Plejaran about them and apparently they also are some sort of evolved intelligent super being made of light!

Let's go deeper down the Rabbit hole.

In Alice in Wonderland there is a famous line by the Cheshire cat!

He says: "Were all mad here!"

Many people have gotten tattoos of it.

However in this reality…

If you go back he will say instead: "Most everyone is mad here!"

All this merchandise that said it the original way still exists!

When there is residue that indicates Dolly should really have braces in Moonraker we have to question seriously why she doesn't in the scientific community rather than writing off this phenomenon as a few long wing nuts.

There IS residue. There IS evidence that it was different before in our reality. We know because there was a commercial for a Visa mini card where the actor for Jaws displays a card for a girl at a cash register who smiles with a big smile of braces to resemble Dolly from the movie!

The Matrix it's self has a Mandela effect example when the Iconic "What if I told you…" we use to make memes with is missing entirely from the movie!

"What if I told you that everything you know is a lie!" –Morpheus

Try to find it…

Judge Judy no longer has the gavel I do!

In this reality Judge Judy has never used a gavel.

Residue of the gavel is found on Family guy and SNL

Parody after parody.

I have seen residue of the Berenstein bears in a short GIF video and on the Simpsons.

People remember a dash in Kit-Kat.

I am not so sure… Mona Lisa has her expression changed? I she smirking more? Grassy background?

My grandma sang Mona Lisa. She also sang Harbor Lights to me before she died.

Do you remember the Monopoly guy having an eye piece? I do. There is residue.

Do you remember the cartoon Looney Tunes or Looney Toons?

Tiny Toons…   indicates the original way.

Max Laughan says he remembers some of his own signatures differently in his notes.

I remember Interview with a Vampire with the letter A not the word the.

Were there 4 people when JFK got shot or 6?

I remember only 4...   bread crumbs indicate four.

Consider if you wanted to alter an important part of history to make the event more ambiguous!   With fractures in time intentionally with some invention perhaps evidence could be buried.

When man monkeys with time we do something drastic and toy with the nature of physics in a way that may have irreversible consequences. With time travel a person may go missing or a group of people may vanish from reality. There is a phenomenon of missing people who vanish our national forests. People go missing...   and sometimes children reappear in a location so far away from where they were before. Alien abduction is one thing but also consider how a tear in the fabric of reality may transport people to other times or locations.

Gil Pérez in 1593 teleported 9000 miles and appeared in Mexico City from Manila.

Whales drop inland full of drugs from the sky according to a seminar with Peter Davenport National UFO reporting center. Peter visited my house once running as a politician and I made a windmill out of his political sign. Like me has probably seen his fair share of UFO photos and footage. Also mentions cases of missing people. Consider if there were time bandits. Consider people altering the past simply by pushing a pen across a table could cause it to land on the floor causing someone to fall and die after leaving a diner. They could be gone before anybody knew what happened. Playing with fields and time reminds me of the life of Al Bielek talking about the Philidelphia Experiment on Art Bell. An elaborate story...

When you play with magnetic field and space time trying to produce an invisibility cloak for your battleship... people ended up stuck in the hull of the ship in agony. Only by jumping off the ship were they able to save themselves ending up in the future in the 80's. It sounds like its strait out of a comic book but we have to take every little note we can. These things and these stories could be lost and even if a few of them are real we have to archive them.

A scientific international archive of experiments 100% disclosed would be nice. We need to know about every experiment ever conducted by man in one place where all black secret projects are also there in.

If the Mandela effect is some gas lighting social experiment you have my attention.

There aren't many things that are able to change a Bible that has been untouched for decades.

If Tom Delonge wants to do some sort of incremental disclosure count me in. In the end it is people like me who are part of the disclosure process when it comes to UFOs. What people like Bob Lazar might have studied at S4 is a physical crat from physical beings so they have something also to offer. Together we conglomerate and tell our stories like the Disclosure project with Steven Greer.

If you haven't seen Sirius I suggest you do so. This is big stuff.

It feels like finally everyone is unified in wanting to get the truth out there in a way that no longer invites mockery but is a serious scientific disclosure of not only UFOs but other phenomenon.

If we are playing god we need to be strait forward about our experiments before they get out of hand. Super weapons and alien technology could get the best of us. We have to learn to keep them out of the hands of fools who might use things like that ad hawk. Yes can antigravity be a blessing? Should we allow high technology to be realized when the World has fractured national military leadership? It is time to come together as a World ARMY to fully understand the nature of strange phenomenon.

The UFO on 9-11 and Yellowstone

I start this chapter with the assumption that you don't believe there was a UFO on 9-11 yet. The vast majority of people are unaware of there being a UFO nearby when the planes hit the towers. I suppose I am the only one with the gust to talk about something that everybody else overlooked. Perhaps as the

Noocracy I see things that the average person doesn't sort of like rain man.

When the first ships came across the ocean the native Americans couldn't believe what they were seeing. They had never seen a ship sail across the ocean before. They were amiss.

Much like summoning a UFO on the ski hill for my mom she couldn't believe what she was seeing. She thought it must be a parasail or something. She couldn't really explain it but that was her best answer. It was a morphing multicolored UFO. They look strange sometimes. I didn't set off some kind of balloon. I'm not like Robert Bingham and his balloon UFOs. She saw it. When I see Robert's UFOs I feel maybe the same way a little. I cannot fathom he would use Mylar balloons like that and try to pass it off as real!   I've had a helicopter checking me out just because I was snowboarding. Maybe I might summon a UFO while it's there? I think anybody almost can summon a UFO with their mind.

The 9-11 UFO was seen from multiple camera angles around New York just after the 1st plane had gone in. A white glowing disk is seen slowly passing off the shot as the 2nd plane its. I mean right as the 2nd plane hits and I am willing to gamble 99.9% of people didn't notice the UFO. See I notice because I'm always looking for them in footage! I know what they look like!

I once had light orbs for The Weather Channel reporting on a complete circular rainbow!

Someday I will show you a photo or a video of the UFOs.

There is something special about this UFO on 9-11 though. I posted a video of a CNN clip where a gray looking orb passes slowly in front of the towers that got a few million hits.

There is a glowing white disk though...

There is a glowing disk floating over a plume of smoke from the base of the building that should not have been there guys!

These UFOs are intelligent!

That is how intelligent they are...

If there were explosions from the base of the building that indicates the explosives used to demo the World Trade Center.

Not only are UFOs saying here we are...

They are attempting to encourage transparency of 9-11?

How cool is that?

All I know is...   Dick Cheney, George W and Benjamin Netanyahu are probably behind it.

The Israeli art students as described by Rebekah Roth explains how there was access to the building integrally.

Everybody knows Jet fuel doesn't melt steal beams and the molten pool that wouldn't go away.

The firefighters got sick from the explosives used.

They were on radio talking about how they could probably tackle the fire just before it blew up.

The firefighters below describe how bombs from the base of the building would go off one by one Boom Boom Boom Boom.

They got blasted out of the base floor.

We could see it was a controlled demolition by the bursts coming out from the sides. Steven E Jones talks about the thermite evidence on video and has smoking gun thermite samples to indicate it was a demolition.

Part of pulling the veil from America is getting them to understand 9-11.

They don't yet understand false flag terrorism to blame a scapegoat enemy of your own desire after attacking yourself.

The idea is that you create a problem... You create the reaction... And then you then promote your solution.

When it comes to predictive cartoons and such the cover of Sesame Street Monsters on the Loose printed in October 1976 takes the boot. Cookie monster is seen taking bites out of what is obviously the twin towers in New York.

Can somebody explain that one? How could 9-11 be planned back as far as 1976?

That is a very long time...

This makes you wonder if time travel is real.

If you wanted to warn about 9-11 from the past with time travel you might infiltrate cartoons and movies in such a way as to predict the event in advance to try to stop it from happening.

Nobody ever thought about the possibility of time travel in relation to 9-11. Stopping it must be important. Talking about it must be important. Somebody somewhere must want me to talk about this stuff because not in a single newspaper or news broadcast or documentary or cartoon did anybody anywhere talk about the UFO on 9-11. Either because they aren't seeing it or because they have a hard time seeing it even when they do see it. It's like trying to get my mom to see a UFO for the 1st time.

She says my grandpa Jack Lael the soar luck cowboy was a person people got quiet and listened to when he talked. She says he had seen a UFO or two himself.

I don't think people have anything to gain from telling lies. The truth is far more interesting than there to be any need for embellishment.

When finally in a World changing event like 9-11 we aren't supposed to talk about the UFO or something?

People feel they would of sounded crazy. It's a serious event and they don't want to be talking about UFOs when it's such a serious event. Well I say hogwash.

There was a fucking UFO and the people who don't see it yet just aren't looking hard enough. Failing to talk about it is a great disservice to humanity. The type of embarrassment means nothing. In the grand scheme of things what is more interesting? A terrorist event made by man or the extraterrestrials watching over it in curiosity?

I say the latter is more important to talk about.

We are being watched my friends.

Whatever we do we should set a good example.

As a planet we need to be moving forwards not backwards.

I actually believe in the mantras of the Obama administration. Stuff like "Forward" and "Yes we can!"

They make people believe in the audacity of hope.

Hope that it really might be confirmed that there is intelligent life in the universe! I think we saw that but maybe people just missed it!

If you ever wanted to know it was official as the highest official in the World I can tell you that yes. People are making contact and yes… people are noticing the crop circles.

I want to have a space mission where we make a welcome mat for Earth that responds to the crop circles we've seen.

Some contain coded messages. Most are simply sacred geometry. Sacred geometry is a means to let us know they are intelligent. What is more intelligent than fractals and sacred geometry? We know the crop circles are real because the manner it is bursts from heat at the node. I have seen footage of light orbs making the crop circles in real time. I suppose it is the typical beings summoned by the few Yahweh summoners. I was once given a book by Mark Ullrich called the Keys of Enoch by James J. Hurtak with YHWH on the front. I find it interesting now that he took time to color the front page and write for the "Adam man."

This book talks about keys that unlock you when the time comes after you see them. I flipped through and saw every key. When you read it however perhaps you are not ready to understand what it is saying. The books is very abstract and I find it peculiar in light of the fact that most what few of us bringing UFOs are calling to Yahweh to bring the lights. If this is the true name of god I am uncertain however the phenomenon may instead be unaffiliated with any religious context.

As a summoner I have a little ring of rocks I stand in.

Prophet Yahweh stood on a little rug sometimes.

I think it is a good idea. Something to make it more obvious that you are intentionally standing in that spot and you are there for a reason.

The orbs of light we have to also consider that they may be the spirits of the dead but energized. They have found a means to energize themselves to make themselves visible light.

With any amount of evidence of life after death we find the most when it comes to wisp style orbs. I call them wisps as from Ultima 7 the Black gate. The wisp who were balls of light in the forest that could talk.

I have to wonder if this isn't instead the deeper reality behind the light orbs. The more faint wisp can be seen like a bubble in a photograph. These bubbles are often seen in photos where people are having fun or at a cemetery. I have a number of them where people are breakdancing on their heads at a hip-hop show in Spokane. In the cemetery also feathery style ectos can sometimes be seen.

I once told my mom that if we go outside and take a picture there would be an orb next to her. Lo and behold as I guaranteed there was a wisp glowing brighter than usual next to my mom. I guess it was just a good guess.

I know my orbs.

I came closer to the conclusion that the orbs might be the spirits of the dead after a long conversation with an Indian friend I played music with where he talked about an elder by the fire he saw stick his arm deep into a boulder and pull it back out again.

With this insight… if this is possible…

As Einstein predicted if we were able to align our molecules correctly we would be able to walk through walls.

This is exactly what the Men who stare at goats tried to accomplish. Mind over matter. Even in our physical form this means we may have the power to also manipulate mater as the orbs do. As corny as it sounds the 1st Earth Battalion idea sounds reminiscent of my aspirations to make a World ARMY. Jim Cannon made a 1st Earth Battalion Operations Manual.

"We organize our future using the omni-centric World wide web. Governments decentralize into Bioregional support centers. We repair our Biosphere using military resources of the world. We create global villages that are multi-ethnic and grow half the food they need nearby. We integrate our industrial energy matrix with nature. We accept only the Aquarian mandate to make fresh water the new gold standard. We open our minds to the new inter-dimensional realities that are emerging. We invite galactic support for our ascension. We see ever more clearly the Golden Age that is in sight. We acknowledge that our planet is qualified to be paradise. We begin with love and lifeforce living. Knowing that levity works as well as gravity and that we can always ask for what we need."

Jim Channon says "Well what we want... My generation says is that we tied this planet together with communications, connections of all sorts. The web... wow and it is unified ethnically. Salute to those guys! Next up, Next generation. Take us to paradise!"

Go planet!

I think its fun to be the new captain planet.

 SNL did a skit where Captain planet goes overkill and zaps everything in sight... even living things to turn them into trees.

I think that is how some hardcore knuckle draggers might view Cascadians.

At Deception falls you can see a few of the old growth trees still alive from the cool of the river after all the other trees burned.

That's how it might be one day. One tree left hanging on by the river. Tree guy is throwing apples and branches at people in a busy downtown Seattle. It's making a fuss... We in our busy lives consider a man climbing a tree a dangerous nuisance. We think he could be a shooter a knee jerk paranoid response. I think of him as kind of an iconic symbol. A guy who is misunderstood is throwing apples and branches that may symbolize our apples getting dumped and our trees getting torched. Probably not that deep... but I'd like to think it is. I like to think that people are really witty. If you look at the good in people instead of the bad we will be a difference society.

When was the last time your climbed a tree?

I climbed trees and had good memories that have since been cut down.

People don't generally care about if climbing a tree is going to be memorable for somebody. We have tight schedules and everybody is in too big of a rush to understand the lives of anyone else. We are too distracted with our own repetitious cycles to see the bigger picture. We are too preoccupied with our own glory than the prospect of contacting star visitors for the 1st time at least in our history. These 1st few contacts are the big ones. They are a trickling before what may one day a be a bustling of an intergalactic traffic hub.

We shouldn't take for granted our opportunities for 1st contact.

Who will best represent planet Earth to an intergalactic body? That is the question we must answer at UNOOSA.

If we allow primitive paranoid nations to have the weapons that bring down space craft we would do ourselves a great disservice. At the highest level nations must fall in line and cooperate so as to not start the spark of an intergalactic conflict. Before real open contact there must be first unity and then a curious diplomacy done with grace.

You don't just go blasting new star visitors because they scare you or because you feel they are an immediate threat to Earth or your national security without talking to 1st contact at UNOOSA. As World general I make the call if there were by a slim chance it go hostile. The #1 on Starcraft gets global battle command. With all our thoughts transparent there is no place for a general to think the old way. Aliens will stop us dead in our tracks predicting all our hostile moves in advance because... Telepathy is real.

The Russians studied telepathy and telekinesis seriously.

What makes you think they don't still today?

Nina Kulagina was famous for moving things with her mind.

You can see her do it. This is a real power people can acquire with sheer focus and willpower.

She is able to move matches across a table...

She can manipulate a compass.

A pop can...

Her heart raced to 180 beats per minute.

The energy field from her living tissue was amplified.

She was able to speed up and slow down the speed of a frogs heart on command. Then was able to stop it's heart.

Could such a power be used against human beings?

Obviously this field deserves more serious study considering the ramifications. One day soon if not already there could be people much more powerful than Nina.

A woman is seen in the forest with her child learning to levitate above her as a man is talking his dog.

There is another phenomenon where telekinetic power is amplified but not from the living but the dead.

In case you haven't realized yet ghosts are real. I am a believer. I was a skeptic once. I have seen too much. Ghost video after ghost video you can see what view as real evidence of the phenomenon. The cameras don't lie. You can tell when special effects are used and when they are not. It is most obvious in the realm of poltergeist telekinesis.

A video you will see happen in multiple circumstances is objects flying about in the kitchen. You will see objects coming in fact from multiple sources simultaneously in a manner that cannot be reproduced with string or special effects. A toaster will fly across the room. Spoons... Plates will break. The table will move. The chairs will all simultaneously separate. Doors will be opening and shutting in multiple locations.

I really want to see Bill Nye the Science guy try to explain this.

There is something I call a Poltergeist Bomb. We are talking about not just objects flying across the room. I am talking about the power of a bomb. This is a PK bomb. It will break all the windows it will deck a person to the floor. It will toss everything in an outward direction like a bubble. You see a ghost can feed on your fear of ghosts to create a PK bomb.

If there was enough fear in one location in a certain instance somehow they are able to take that same fear and blast it kinetically. You don't hear about this stuff from the military only from the Noocracy. We have to be our own disclosure. We have to disclose information we know others don't have.

It is our duty to end government secrecy across the board. I think there isn't an area where people can't handle the truth. Technical weapons data may however be omitted.

The movie Push came complete with the theme of Pushers, Watchers and screamers. The future man will have powers we could never have imagined. On planet Erra nearly all people use telepathy how we use cell phones apparently. I've never been there. I am staying right here on Earth. I am going down with the ship and hopefully we can all prevent that by being more tolerant in our national disputes.

Protecting the planet from asteroids should be the forefront of our research as all it takes is one to slip through and sadly they are much more capable and elusive in a World without real international control of space.

We intend to have a Planetary Defense officer in the Planetary Defense Coordination Office. This person would grow quickly to hate their job if an asteroid slipped through to destroy a city. I would hate myself if we were not prepared to detour dangerous near earth objects. We need more satellites on the opposite side of our solar system to see asteroids that would otherwise blind side us. Asteroids as a weapon must not be tolerated. Simply bombing them can be dangerous. My idea is to push them with rockets. You can shoot a rocket that attaches to the NEO and kick it out of range. Part of being responsible for the planet starts 1st with asteroid deflection. We may have been given a free ride when it comes to things like that without knowing it. Extraterrestrials are here to help but we shouldn't count on them for anything just like we shouldn't count on America anymore in Cascadia. It's time to grow up.

We all have to take part in making our planet as safe as possible when we are in an era of dangerous advancements.

Lindley Johnson is a near earth object specialist at NASA's Planetary Science Division in Washington. This officer will play a leading role in coordinating interagency and intergovernmental efforts in response to any potential impact threats.

"The formal establishment of the Planetary Defense Coordination Office makes it evident that the agency is committed to perform a leadership role in national and international efforts for detection of these natural impact hazards, and to be engaged in planning if there is a need for planetary defense," said Johnson.

For the 1st time in history we are looking at what could be considered an alien megastructure near a star called KIC 8462852 1,500 light years away in the constellation Cygnus.

Astronomers are unable to explain the dimming light fluctuations and many seem to think that it may be an alien megastructure. If such a structure exists it is a very large undertaking. To Micio Kaku "this star is breaking all the rules." And "we would have to rewrite astronomy textbooks."

A massive object seems to be blocking this particular star. On star Trek we have seen structures like The Borg and Deep space 9. We have to consider a new type of civilization that perhaps builds a massive space station instead of inhabiting a planet.

It might make sense. Eventually the Earth may overpopulate and build into space. I myself desire to build the 1st orbital city. This is a much more ambitious undertaking than mere space tourism. We can build a city and we can do it by changing how we get to space and what we put up there. Bigelow aerospace for example is building expandable habitats that don't require rigid frames for possible space habitation. Thinking outside the box conglomerating the ideas of all our space agencies we can accomplish more than if we all just do our own thing.

Once upon a time in Popular Science we had ideas of our own to build a large shield half way between the sun and the Earth.

If we build such a shield to combat dangerous solar radiation in the future from destroying the Earth it would have to be a similarly massive undertaking. Other ides included having ships around the equator that throw a fine mist into the air.

When UFOs are flying over something we should take notice.

Of recently I saw a cluster of orbs over Yellowstone volcano. We should not overlook this. This is a super volcano...

I have not been very scared of it but when UFOs appear I become more concerned. They want us to pay attention right now.

"This is the highest number of earthquakes at Yellowstone within a single week in the past five years, but is fewer than weekly counts during similar earthquakes swarms in 2002, 2004, 2008 and 2010."

We have had more since June...

I have previously warned about man made Earthquakes over Yellowstone. This is almost a peculiar swarm of quakes to me. The number of them is off the charts. My hope is that the caldera being so huge that that the circumference is inhibiting to a pyroclastic explosion. When volcanoes this big go we have to be prepared once again for the prospect of an ice age because that size of a blast could cool the Earth as the ashes wrap over the jet stream clouding our sun. Without sun that means we have to endure the cold with hydrogen from snow and grow plants with LED lights.

"Since the most recent giant caldera-forming eruption, 640,000 years ago, approximately 80 relatively nonexplosive eruptions have occurred. Of these eruptions, at least 27 were rhyolite lava flows in the caldera, 13 were rhyolite lava flows outside the caldera and 40 were basalt vents outside the caldera. Some of the eruptions were approximately the size of the devastating 1991 Pinatubo eruption in the Philippines, and several were much larger. The most recent volcanic eruption at Yellowstone, a lava flow on the Pitchstone Plateau, occurred 70,000 years ago. "

So the answer is that it is capable of both lava flows as well as pyroclastic explosions. If it is the latter the entire continent could see something we and possibly the whole world is not ready for. I have looked at how deep it goes under the Earth and it has an incredible amount of lava beneath it. It is larger than expected now that we can image it.

"During the three giant caldera-forming eruptions that occurred between 2.1 million and 640,000 years ago, tiny particles of volcanic debris (volcanic ash) covered much of the western half of North America, likely a third of a meter deep several hundred kilometers from Yellowstone and several centimeters thick farther away. Wind carried sulfur aerosol and the lightest ash particles around the planet and likely caused a notable decrease in temperatures around the globe."

From the map it appears that Cascadia is just out of range of the last explosion. It goes from North Dakota to Texas. It takes out the eastern side of Montana and is inhibited by the Rocky Mountains. South eastern Idaho gets hit... If you draw a line from there to Southern California. Everything from LA to just east of Texas in Louisiana gets hit by the blast. Then back up from there to Montana crossing over everything inside of that and between.

List of states likely affected by a similar Yellowstone blast:

Montana

North Dakota

South Dakota

Idaho

Wyoming

Nevada

Utah

Colorado

Nebraska

Kansas

Minnesota

Iowa

Missouri

Oklahoma

Arizona

New Mexico

Texas

Arkansas

Louisiana

Those are the states that are in danger the next time
Yellowstone goes.

If scientists tell you that they think it's going to go if I were in
those states I would move or take a long vacation...

You see. We have a tenancy to just duke it out and build entire
cities in dangerous regions of the globe.

Take the entire east coast...   The Gulf of Mexico...

The Bahamas... Cuba and Puerto Rico.

All of you guys are in a location where Hurricanes occur on a
regular basis! Get out of there! Look at the hurricane path
maps. You may change your mind about living there.

It's not going to let up! Hurricanes will occur in that area on a
regular basis and you have to learn to adapt as people.

Sometimes people have to just learn to move from an entire
region or they will be hit with redundant disasters.

Or just stay there and turn the Gulf of Mexico into your big
fracking toilet...

Fracking is banned in Cascadia. It ruins the ground water.

The obsolete power grid and the future of flight

The power grid... It's obsolete. It should of never went up and it
is a hazard to the future era of flight!

I want everybody like Cathy Mcmorris Rodgers to get a clue
when it comes to protecting Hydropower and the power grid.

First off Nikola Tesla wanted wireless electricity not a huge high amp hazard over our heads. I want you all to take this back to Tesla and Westinghouse. Westinghouse wanted a power meter to make money selling people electricity because he is a cold blooded business man. Tesla on the other hand who gave us everything from Radio to Alternating current wanted free energy for everyone done wirelessly...

This ties back to everything that is wrong with America people.

We put profit over innovation.

What a huge mistake. Someone in my own family was hit with the main lines as a lineman. He survived but only one in 11 do. That shit will roast your body in one hand and out your foot.

Have you ever electrocuted a pickle to see it glow inside?

That's what happens to your body...

We are mass manufacturing a web of electric death over our own heads like idiots. It is the Idiocracy who made this web not Tesla. We are to this day fumbling to understand this man.

Only now are we discovering wireless electricity again.

I want to tell politicians that they are behind the times in the stone age. They think they are smart. They think they know electricity and electrical engineering.

Who does the Public Utility District call when they want someone to wire their own building?

My family... Brisbine Electric has been wiring most of Wenatchee since 1947.

Who does the Saddle Rock gold mine trust with their security to find out who is stealing gold? My dad set up the cameras in Brisbine Electric.

The family business it's self is tied to the power grid yet I am here to tell you as president of a new country it has too many amps. We want to mass produce home power so everyone can have power independently from the grid.

I will tell you why it is important.

People need to learn how to control their own power financially when we have these problems with Avista gouging people who don't even use their house on vacation. They are billing people without checking the meter whatever they feel like possibly based on previous data. They have been caught overbilling construction sites. The people hate them and their monopoly over the grid. That is one thing...

I am talking about how in a storm how powerlines drape to the ground and a child walking down the street might get hit with the amps of Rocky Reach dam walking through a puddle. It's not even that...

People aren't generally afraid of it YET.

I used to have dreams about trying to fly through a maze of power lines. I have many dreams that I could fly but ended up fearful of hitting tower built to the sky with a live wire. We just end up building the wires higher and higher and keep adding more and more. This is crazy. In 3rd World countries you can see how crazy electricity gets when the wires start cluttering between buildings. This is the type of World we are creating.

Something stupid is now smart in a 3ʳᵈ World country and the World has mass produced power grids flying cables with helicopters across the land. But… We don't want it.

It is a waste of metal. It is a high voltage hazard for the future of flight because in the future. We will be taking off from our front yards. We will have man sized quadcopters that will have to avoid all these power lines. The old politicians aren't remembering Tesla and they aren't thinking of the future either.

 They are just thinking about making money and looking good.

Is there a way to have power at home?

Yes…

We can make power from crystal cells. Solid electrolyte batteries like crystal cells are a solution. They can be made at home when you put a galvanized bolt into a copper pipe without touching it to the sides filled with a salt based solid electrolyte. You will need to melt Epsom salt, No salt alternative and Alum in equal parts into each cell. Once you get 12 volts make another 12 volt battery cell pack and another and another to get your amps up. Connect it to a power inverter when you get 15 amps and you just made your 1ˢᵗ home circuit!

Like Stanly Meyer building the water car to fight big oil we can do the same by ditching the power grid with alternative energy concepts. When people giant wind turbines spread across land with housing people complain about the wooshing sound and talk about health effects. It seems like the people in the documentary Down Wind are just milking it getting emotional. If it's a problem though I just solved it.

Just because we have a new way of doing things doesn't always make it better. The original pile battery by Alessandro Volta has more potential and is much cleaner than a Sulfuric acid battery. These first batteries were the real revelation.

Although they had low amps this is the type of battery that has stood the test of time. By stacking zinc and copper disks with a brine soaked electrolyte we create the 1st battery.

The Oxford Electric Bell is such a battery built in 1840. That battery is similar but covered in a tree resign or Sulphur to contain it's moisture. That bell has been ringing a bell behind two layers of glass for 177 years!

John Bedini used Rochelle salt for his crystal cell.

John Hutchison who made a bowling ball float in the air using surplus electronics and sports a Star Trek suit for shits and giggles also made a crystal cell where he hilariously grabbed a handful of dark rocks that look like Andesite from some public landscaping to crush into his cell. Perhaps a difference in minerals is similar to garnering electricity with anode and cathode metals. Some people also add grinded Pyrite.

I guess fools gold might be more useful than real gold?

For the future of flight I suggest creating a generator using water fracture but instead using the hydrogen to directly power the engine we use it to power a generator to power instead electric motors so that the quadcopter hybrid plane can last longer in the air. The batteries on board will add to its safety if the fuel runs out and adding a high elevation hydrogen balloon above the craft we can also increase its efficiency and safety. If the batteries run out the balloon will keep it in the air and if the balloon pops it will be so high it won't hurt the people inside and the battery water flight can take over. There would be no need for a parachute unless both the balloon and the batteries failed.

So yes... In spite of the Hindenburg crashing in flames we should bring back airships and make them safer. If the explosion happens above us it won't matter and we can parachute. The Hindenburg had a flammable coating on the balloon. People were stupid and many flights have already happened over the ocean we just forgot about airships because of one incident. We should make them better instead of abandoning them for planes and helicopters. Perfecting airships is the key to the future of firefighting. How can we carry the amount of water I desire without airships with blades and thrusters?

We don't need to use helium if we just separate the distance between the crew and the balloon.

I want to automate firefighting in the sky.

A grid of drones may now manifest because we have discovered how to make them fly in perfect formation without hitting one another. With this grid of drones I am able to lift more water from the river using scaled up quadcopters running on hydrogen. We can now let the grid see where the hottest parts of the mountain are and focus on that location single file our double file or quadra file. Automating the sky with such a grid is also the wet dream for the military industrial complex they haven't yet realized. Sure I could revolutionize the military too but now that I am World general and national war is over what need is there to militarize? Only when facing a hostile alien encounter should the Noocracy be dedicated to the feat of sharpening its sword.

We should all be so good as to not give the government another atom bomb in the face of national paranoia. World War II was a different time. A competitive time for physical domination.

I see nothing wrong with the TV show battle bots.

To my generation we would rather fight with giant robots in the ocean like Voltron or Pacific Rim with no people killed. Friendly military competition is something I would like to encourage among the nations.

We have an Olympics for sports...

Now we will have the Olympics of our military prowess.

Like how the UFC helps keep people from street fighting.

There is a more honorable way to fight without weapons.

In a more civilized World I challenge you all to do your experimental national fighting on Venus for the time being.

Earth is too special to contaminate with weapons fighting in the ocean. This is our only home. We have no alternative and we may not have one for many years. If you would like to change that part of the process is making the World ARMY fully realized. Fractured leadership is irrational and irresponsible.

There must be no question who the leader of Earth is and what must be done to make this planet a better place. I will stop annual marine slaughter and I will stop oil spills. I will stop forest fires and deforestation. I don't like tar sands. We shouldn't ruin the land. We shouldn't contaminate it with radiation. We shouldn't contaminate it with our left over bio-weapons and chemical weapons. A World ARMY has to be established to keep America from being a bully if we become one or any nation.

The truth is hard for people to swallow.

One man can start a new nation.

You can if you understand the Declaration of Independence!

There may be a Cascadian movement but as far as there being a nation state I did it on my own. I did it by having a will of steel.

I did it by knowing what is right and wrong …

I did it by knowing correct from incorrect...

If he was the smartest man in the World you have to consider that maybe that person deserves to be leader more than the one you elected in your TV Reality show popularity contest. Rich people win that contest not poor people. You have to swallow the reality that just because someone like Bill Gates is rich doesn't mean they are on the right side of history in every respect when looking at the prospect of manipulated human population control. He may want to be responsible in his own way but it may be the wrong way. Cathy Mcmorris Rodgers may think kinetic hydropower is amazing but that doesn't mean we shouldn't consider breaking some of the Snake River dams for the dwindling Salmon. The Natives want something like that done. At the very least we should consider tearing one down as a symbol that we are willing to change.

Chemical hydro power is technically superior to putting a dam on the entire river. You don't need a river to make chemical hydropower. We could have made turbines spin in a linear fashion instead of blocking the entire river. I think people know how I feel about Nuclear energy. Although my grandpa Waldo Brisbine learned how to do electrical as an apprentice at Hanford that doesn't mean I want 9 nuclear reactors in my region. I certainly don't want any more in the post Fukushima World that Light Forms warned me about. If I someone has a real message from space like mine I want the leader of Earth to be able to hear it. We have a serious problem with communication in this regard. Although we have the World Wide Web the powers that be have a problem listening to both the people they represent and the scientific community. I would like to see that change with Cascadia. I don't like someone representing me that is afraid to communicate back. I don't think we can afford that anymore. Oil is dying and Coal is over. Coal is the one energy I can stomp my foot down and say without question that this is the height of human stupidity. It's not about jobs it's about people having the right jobs. Do you really want to be responsible for a career that is bringing down this planet? Are you really going to just take that check and say "Fuck you World... I have a family at home!"

That is the attitude. You could be that nurse injecting unwitting children with mercury. You could be that doctor that is complicit with giving babies autism. It has been going on since the 1930s when we started playing with Mercury. That is the culprit.

Are you going to be complicit with the aluminum industry even if they contaminate the landscape with it from the sky and pump their waste into our water?

I built a new thermal generator you can put in your window or on the gas stove...   I made the Brisbine drive. I did something.

We should all do something. Make a penny pile and shave one side for its copper and zinc! Lincoln would be proud!

The power of the internet and compartmentalization

The internet has changed the World we know. Has it been a good thing? Yes. Is it a double edge sword? Yes it is.

Who controls it? Can it be controlled?

I was one of the 1st people in Wenatchee to put Fiber optic in my home with Panda Computers. Andy the owner when you walk in is a big fat guy who knows allot about computers. I would marvel at the huge ancient hardrive he had. The fact that we can do all this is wild. Did we learn about computers from aliens?

Even I have questions that cannot easily be answered in 2017.

I have to question the existence of time travel when the 1st home computer the Adam computer was named after me. I have a stockpile of such coincidences I archive on Facebook.

Fiber optic is connected to my house...

It wasn't easy to get it connected. It was technical and over the phone with Andy. Everything runs through ICANN.

One third of the people on the planet have the internet...

That means if you have a message for the Whole world they aren't necessarily going to hear it. At best one out of three people would hear it so if the sky was falling two out of three people might not hear about it till they plug in or tune in. Should we really care though? People who quit using it describe their lives improving sometimes.

Consider also we are a people that now sit too much.

We are actually meant to be standing most of the day and shouldn't spend over 4 hours sitting. Taking care of your back affects your whole body. When you sit too much you make your back weaker and weaker until one day you have horrific back pain after you lift something. You shouldn't lift heavy things if you have been glued to the internet for long durations.

If you are on the internet allot you should reposition your computer so you are standing instead.

If we are plugged in we have a social connection at least we think we do. Often studies show that socially it has backfired causing rifts between friends and family over things like technical differences politically. For instance telling my uncle that I am the president of the west coast in front of his friends annoys him enough that he is willing to block me to prevent being embarrassed by his nephew. An unelected president would surely be a cruel despot in our knee jerk reaction.

I myself who do not tend to block people for their differing opinions I am openly willing to spark up in all types of conversations. I who desire free speech across the board blocked my own brother for being redundantly belittling and disrespectful to me. He cannot handle it. I have insulted his intellect and called him stupid so he feels compelled to outwit the World's smartest person at every corner attempting to attack the soundness of my mind and my character.

I once had another type of brother who would of done the opposite. He wrote a paper on Mars in collage. It was his pride and joy. He also wrote about the atrocities of the US government and would surely instead be proud of me for starting a new country. Such things are certainly more meaningless now that he is gone. Jacob Jefferson (Anti-Bush) Brisbine was someone

special. He would of wanted his name said like that or
Palindrome like BocaJacoB.
What good is the internet if I can't show you his band
Jabberwocky from Highs chool?

My brother was the next Jim Morrison.

They sounded like the Doors had a baby… when they were in
fucking High School.

He was a poet.

We live in a World where they have all but died off…

On the internet you will see our language has been reduced to
meaningless efficiency when saying acronym's like LOL.

ROFL is not a word… But if you have been on the internet awhile
you will understand its important meaning.

We don't make what websites are popular do we?

We have to buy that traffic that someone else controls…

To be heard a person will have to invest real money to be heard
in 2017. You cannot simply have incredible information or
entertainment and expect it to have any fan base.

We who do not pay are like ghosts.

As a rap artist for years now I have been GHOST PERSON.

I am here to say that the World's smartest person no matter
what they do or accomplish in life may be unlikely to reach the
World with a message from outer space like…

"DO NOT PUNISH"

Facebook desires to expand their reach with a solar plane and I can't help but be inspired. I myself however don't agree with compartmentalization or censorship of the news. There could be a point where to simulate that Facebook is open and connected globally 30 people are paid to comment in a foreign language in a group to make you believe so.

Your reach social reach may be compartmentalized by the CIA integrating with things like social networking. Facebook having such facial recognition is no accident. Such facial recognition can be eventually integrated into a super surveillance grid that allows people to see things like a terrorist when they log in.

Terrorists who are still dumb enough to try to and recruit people with social networking will now be easy prey.

We must consider that the popularity of people is maintained and controlled by ultimately assassination. If someone is a ding bat in the brain perhaps they may be allowed to be popular as there is no threat to national security.

Is Cascadia a threat to national security?

The way I see it... it is in the best interests for America to allow it because it protects the homeland from foreign attack. It confuses the prospect of foreign invasion. However as much as they would like me to be fully integrated into the US government I am not. I am what they call a lone Wolf. At best to them at this point I am a fruit cake to be lazily monitored by the NSA.

If you use Facebook messenger on your cell phone all speech may be monitored. If you have smart devices you are openly bringing the latest 1984 technology into your home.

Your cell phone will even have independent wiring to the battery so your conversations can be heard. Your laptop camera can be accessed so people tape over it as you may have seen in the movie Snowden.

Think of a room with a 1000 screens like the architect has in the Matrix and you will get the picture. Omnipresent surveillance is here. Under the guise of fighting terrorism it is reaching the far corners of the globe.

Obama says:

"Basically I am here to announce that we are building Iron Man... I'm gonna blast off in a second! This is a secret project we've been working on for a long time. Not really... Maybe! It's classified!"

Well I would say yes very soon.

Think of Iron Man Vs the Terrorists in the Gulmira fight scene.

This may only be a movie for now but when the Military sees something like this they take notice. Fictional characters like Iron Man may inspire them. Everything comes first from the mind before it is manufactured. When it comes to the mass manufacture of killer robots I want there to be a World ARMY under my command before it happens. Who else can I trust with leadership when legions of killer robots on are on the horizon.

The military is more apt to use robots than people in the future because their guys don't die and a robot can already be programmed to be 100 times more accurate.

We risk the near and present danger that such robots may fall into the wrong hands or a rouge nation who has lost its temper. Just one might take out an entire city.

These robots fall into the category of super weapons.

Already you can watch Boston Dynamics with a robot that is doing back flips. Biped robots are here and they are here to stay. The balance is nearly perfect. With perfect balance next are the weapons they mount.

When I have a dream that seems like aliens are telling me that I get killed by an armored hovering drone with a Gatling gun I start to pay attention. It makes me question if it is my own mind or a message.

To prepare for nasty drones we must all as nations research the latest anti drone technology. We shouldn't let them come near heads of state or airports. It should be standard policy in 2017.

Sky Wall looks good.

Trained hawks look ok.

Drone defender can bring them down by aiming at them and pointing them to the ground.

House Bill 912 called to outright ban drones in the state of Texas.

We live in the post handgun drone World and people don't like them anymore. However there is still much enthusiasm when it comes to the prospect of using them for delivery.

Amazon is a very big player and they desire to deliver packages with drones as a standard. Perhaps we could soon be fully acclimated to seeing them all around us.

It really depends on if we let fear get the best of us. It really depends on the paranoia of the government. Now in the case of Cascadia I myself do not want drones flying around me. I just told you I had a nightmare about it.

However for everyone else I cannot speak for them on this matter. Maybe they want to have packages delivered faster and are willing to trade their security for faster packages.

Franklin said; "They who would give up an essential liberty for temporary security, deserve neither liberty or security."

Perhaps I should just accept the more efficient way of doing things. I predict such packages may also be attacked by birds causing delivery to fail. Batteries will run out.. Packages will be too heavy. I am not so sure Amazon is thinking this one through. Given the fact that they want us to trust them with the key to our houses all this is a bit much and encroaching. Drones can both be both a weapon and a tool for security. On some scale they may be viable to deliver small packages. With the internet we are able to buy such packages with greater ease from huge retailer that doesn't really care if it cuts out small business or steps all over our personal bubble of space with drone packages. Jeff Bezos although the richest man doesn't understand or care about the mindset of Chief Seattle who is far wiser than us. Buying land is easy for him and it is easy for him to gentrify the Seattle when he buys real estate. When a person is that rich we owe it to ourselves to teach them the Native American way of thinking where people are all equally generous instead of trying to get as much for themselves as possible.

This land is your land... This land is my land...

I am not going to sing it. We want to make our own songs now but you get the picture. When Thanksgiving comes around if we are to learn anything from the Natives it should be the joy of giving. The fact that there is higher joy in giving is something we need to learn as a people because we don't understand that. No matter how many things we buy for ourselves it won't be enough with the American mindset. I am not saying to tax the rich and create socialism. I am saying educate the rich and let the good provide donations instead of taxing. We may be a poor government but we will be one that is good and on the right side of history. Inspire the rich to be good instead of stealing from them. If you steal from them they become no better as people.

The rich will give again and that is my hope with the Republic of Cascadia. Reaching them may prove difficult.

The more rich people get the harder they are to reach. Politicians and celebrities are very difficult to communicate with. Just because we have social media doesn't mean they hear us when we try to chat. Perhaps they may one day have a filter to filter out the poor. They reside in their own psycho bubble of bliss and pomposity.

Compartmentalization may happen in a variety of ways.

A person who is too political may now be filtered out. Only if you are talking about a fun time at the park with balloons and laughter are people allowed to see what you do. Much like in Black Ceiling we all struggle to show a fake happy face and make fake happy friends to be popular. We all have a white picket fence and everything is perfect. If we video our new car that is great! Advertising and car culture feel important. To social networks like Facebook video sharing like Youtube websites are bought out and often compromised or now sensor videos to more appeal sponsors. Every video must be Disney friendly or it no longer is allowed to be popular. The people who told you swear words are bad and not the people who tell you that have taken hold. Such political correctness is ironically incorrect for subjugating people into separate classes based on if they key words like Fuck, Shit and Cunt or wearing a tie.

George Carlin said;

"Political correctness is America's newest form of intolerance, and it is especially pernicious because it becomes disguised as tolerance. It presents itself as fairness, yet attempts to restrict and control people's language with strict codes and rigid rules. I'm not sure that's the way to fight discrimination. I'm not sure silencing people or forcing them to alter their speech is the best method for solving problems that go much deeper than speech."

Myspace bulletins was the 1st place people really had free flowing information about the World springing up. New information that people had not been hearing for decades. Some call it the truth movement. Well that movement was squashed when Rupert Murdock bought Myspace.

We had our own custom portal for HTML code injection allowing people to be more streamline about how they portray themselves to the World. Special photos and videos or text or an Mp3 player could be inserted unlike Facebook. The truthers could be found in the bulletins. Bulletin after bulletin exposing the money masters are and who controls the media. Every conspiracy theory was fresh and alive for discussion. When a fat cat buys the hub of social media it moves. It moves to facebook where our dumb family members have conglomerated. We are helplessly subject to using anti-social media to express ourselves.

With a new country and a clean slate however…

We have an opportunity to make a new hub for social media where free speech is a very real thing. We are on the cusp of a great censorship. RT has become one of the last bastions for journalism. Now RT America has had to register as a Russian agent. Google considers RT Russian propaganda. Of all places one that has people like Larry King and Jesse Ventura is being compartmentalized in search engines.

Jesse Ventura had a show on Tru TV called Conspiracy Theory. The show has covered topics from detention centers in the US to 9-11. It had an episode about water… It was about how we are selling water from the Great lakes to China. I see nothing wrong with sharing water. However I have a problem when it is being done by corporations under our noses when they guzzle a lake dry I am going to want to be the President.

People working on special projects and study are also compartmentalized. The left hand never sees what the right hand is doing because when it comes to secret projects being social is the last thing the military wants when it is trying to protect secrets from foreign nations. Today I am trying to say that such secrecy endangers us. It ramps up a cold war with governments. It causes governments to race to have the latest weapons and they will hack and insert spies for espionage to find out every secret. Everybody has the incentive to be the best but what are we trying to be the best at? The best at making weapons… Tools of death… That does not encourage the World's civilizations to prosper.

What are we the best at? Suppressing people and information.

Don't mix family with business or Government

Have you ever heard the saying?

"Don't mix family with business?"

Family and business don't mix because when you have a
business you are always trying to make the maximum profit. This
drive for a business to make the money possible has ruined us
mentally. In the generation of our parents they brag about how
rich their children are. That is their measure of success. That is
what this culture of consumerism has accomplished. None of
them really seem to care about how they got rich. Perhaps a
richer child brings the more stable nursing home experience they
long for. This blue collar animosity that the working class has will
need to go when our jobs are lost to automation and robots. For
instance Amazon who is squashing out allot of small business
competition has a good side in that they are very reliable due to
this automating process. When someone in the mail room at
USPS steals my laptop in San Francisco and I get no reciprocation
I am upset with the mail system. I would prefer Amazon took
over the mail because they are more reliable and robots aren't
going to steal my packages. Their stock probably just went up
just saying that. When they wanted to make a second base to
expand their business I think it's funny that they went to
Vancouver BC. Every mayor begged for a piece of Amazon and
nobody in the states got it. I just have to laugh. Do you want your
city to have reduced romance and gentrification?

My parent's generation clearly cares more about business than
family. I have felt like that sometimes. I took care of my
quadriplegic brother in a World that felt he was too much of a
burden till his last breath. Not that I wanted any of his money

when he died but my dad got it all a 100 thousand or something.
Well my brother said he would of gave allot of it to my niece and
nephew. Nobody cared about his actual wishes when he died.
Nobody is going to listen to me about what Jacob wanted. He
wanted us to snort his ashes with a hallucinogen when he died.
That is what the truth is. My dad went on vacations and spent
only 40 grand of it to help buy us a house back in Wenatchee. I
say this because I want to tell you what our parents are really
like for Xennials. We paid rent on the house for 4 years or so
then my dad decided he wanted us to buy it. While I am working
in the family business mind you...   He wants me to buy the same
house he got for 40 grand for 180 grand and to take out a loan
for it. My X-wife was fine with the idea but the whole thing got
on my nerves. That's not how I am going to treat my children.

My dad is so into that business mentality he is looking to make a
buck off his own children as if I am too stupid to notice. I love
my dad but I need to tell the World that this is how it is for our
entire generation.

This is why they say not to mix business and family.

Now I want you all to come to the realization that there aren't
enough of us to take care of you guys in the nursing home.

Walt Disney said:

"A man should never neglect his family for business."

I want our generation to be instead the one that builds a house
for their children like actual parents instead of just being land
lords that make us buy the same house for 5 times what they
bought it for.

We carry our children into the future we don't rip them off till
we die. I would much rather have a father that cared more about
me while I'm alive than one who wills me some portion of money
after he dies.
Our parents should be the type to help us build our homes not
kicking us out at 18 after we help them build their homes.

We have to come to the terms that their entire generation has
lost its way in this regard. You can see it in how the politicians
care for the homeless. They don't. Not really.

The government treats the homeless as subhuman. Around the
nation homeless have even been known to vanish. Perhaps they
are taken to a detention center never to be seen again and no
one notices because their friends and family have all forgotten
them.

If corporations are protected like the US protected Monsanto
with the Monsanto protection act it does nothing when
Washington attempts to sue over the Spokane River.

"The lawsuit, filed last week in U.S. District Court in Spokane,
alleges that the company sold chemicals that it knew for decades
were a danger to people and the environment..."

The city will have to spend 300 million to clean up
polychlorinated biphenyls.

"Monsanto knew that PCBs would contaminate water supplies,
would degrade marine habitats, would kill fish species, and
would endanger birds and animals," the complaint says.

This is what happens when you mix business with government.

A corporation like Monsanto becomes backed by the most powerful government in the World and is impervious to lawsuits when the people realize a chemical weapons manufacturer has chemically altered our entire landscape.

Congress actually banned PCBs already.

Monsanto was the sole producer of PCBs between 1935 and 1979, when Congress banned them. The chemicals, developed by Monsanto as a coolant in electrical transformers and capacitors, were used in many products, including paint, hydraulic fluids, sealants and ink. According to the lawsuit, Monsanto learned by the 1930s that the chemicals were toxic, but it continued making them and concealed the danger from government officials.

Perhaps we should use Evans coolant instead of things like PCBs and anti-freeze. If you put it in a car it never boils so your engine never overheats.

Other cities have similarly sought damages from Monsanto over PCB pollution, including San Diego and San Jose, California, and Westport, Massachusetts.

We are all in the same boat. When government and business mix we get fracking ruining the ground water in state after state. For some places it's already too late. They can't get their water back.

Josh Fox Director of "Gasland" was arrested attempting to film a hearing on Fracking because he didn't have proper "credentials."

He says that "This is a public hearing and I am well within his 1st amendment rights and I am being taken out."

This shows you the true nature of what happens when you want to talk about the government being in bed with Fracking.

They are going to make the Gulf of Mexico a giant Fracking toilet.

We literally have a toilet in the ocean now. That is how we are thankful for our planet.

From Ohio, Defiance county my mother's great grandfather, John Putter and Wife Lillie Purtee buried at the cemetery at Almira, were pioneers of the Grand Coulee Dam area and wanted to leave Ohio to come west. He woke up in the middle of the night and said that there is something wrong with the water and they headed west with their family.

Many headed west in the days of the dust bowl.

The dust bowl is a prime example of why we need to be more adaptive to climate change. There is still climate change going on even before the days ambiguous super weapons capable of creating drought. So you see there is still the same incentive for us to be better at adapting for our own survival. Namely we need to adapt better to the cold and extreme drought.

A weapon that creates drought like HAARP we should be concerned about also such things being misused to be create cold. If you are able to open a temporary portal from space with no atmosphere that means a super freeze weapon could be created as well by sharing space temperature with the ground. Even when building a city in orbit we risk being exposed to the vacuum of space. At the lowest space can be 2.7 degrees above -459.67 F. The only way to get heat is through photons. On the cold side in orbit we are able to get -212 F. Now if we were able to share that -212 with the ground it could deep freeze a city and we would just be wondering why nature is being so cruel to us.

In the era of weather weapons aside from manmade tornadoes, earthquakes and tsunamis we must also consider that the cold might also be used against us.

The cold already freezes our crops every year. If we get a late freeze or an early freeze an entire garden or field of food will die in the open. All it would take is one freeze at an odd time to destroy the crops of a nation.

 In the case of cattle ranchers nobody has been through it more than my grandpa Jack Lael from Northport Washington where he was dubbed as the "World's most weather beaten cowboy."

The weather beaten title came from Madisonville Texas by the Sidewalk Cattle-men's association. For seven weeks the temperature stayed below zero except one day when it rose 12 above.

The cows started dropping their calves...

He described how an ice sickle would form from the cow's nose and accumulate all the way to the ground.

"I saved all I could on canned milk."

After the World hearing about it they took him to Texas in 1949.

In an article "Poke" looking for rich widow." It says Jack Lael, 26 a cowpoke from Northport, Wash, stepped off air lines as eleven pretty cowgirls tried to kiss him. Evidently they showered him with women and he got to date Miss America for nursing his heard of 276 cattle during the severe blizzard. Even down in

Texas a likely jealous rancher Tom Arnett described his days of cold. "One winter 30-odd years ago I rode up what I thought was a hill. I looked down and my horse was standing on the backs of hundreds of frozen cattle.

Now when animals get cold in the old days of the natives they would migrate and be nomadic. But since we have become so territorial with our gates and our property and our barb wire fences we have altered the landscape for migrating animals. I want you all to think of that when you have cattle in a blizzard. The cattle themselves would be warmer if they were allowed to freely roam south. We wouldn't even have cattle in fact we would have Bison. In cowboy slang back in the day then they'd call a fake cowboy a "Gunsil" and a real one a "Waddy" I think a real Waddy these days would be a Guy on a Buffalo.

When I think of the Buffalo I think of the real reason why we need a new government. How obtuse it is for Barack Obama to name Bison as the national mammal after attempting to confront him about how federal agents are just shooting them for no reason to this day. I am sure there is a reason. There is always a reason... But it might be one that they just make up and pull out of their ass.

When I think of the Bison I think of that enormous pile of skulls when the white man killed the Buffalo to intimidate the Indian. I think of how cruel the government must be and how arrogant to do such a thing especially when to this day they are hiring people to shoot Bison.

To this very day we see it in an article on USA today...

"Good with a gun? National Park Service wants your help thinning Grand Canyon bison herd"

Now why would we still want to "thin the heard" after atrocity like that?

If I were a native American and I read that headline I would be thinking that the white man hasn't changed to this very day. We haven't listened to a single word about the sanctity of life the natives tried to teach us.

 Those Bison are the real cattle of this continent.

Those Bison are built to endure the cold better than our cows. We are stupid to kill them. They may one day be our only hope for survival in the cold and you are killing them just because you don't like their numbers so high. How foolish. Their numbers could never be high enough!

My beef with cattle ranchers today is that they don't like the competition of the buffalo. They claim that the buffalo have a disease they don't really have called Brucellosis. This gives them the right to shoot Buffalo where they stand?

The evidence that they even have the disease is fleeting.

Calling them America's national mammal while they do this is a shot in the dark. This twisted trolling America does is much like talking about Hanford and making it a national park when it's a contaminated dirty bomb wet dream. On my 1st album cover you can see men just dumping barrels of radioactive waste down a ravine.

Am I thankful for all America has given me? Yes I am.

But in contrast I feel we could be doing better. Allot better and I don't think the white man has ever come to terms with its history of genocide and slavery. Even when it comes to animals I think the average American is clueless when they see poachers in the news killing all our elk and bears. People just think it's random red necks who like to kill stuff. Only the Noocracy considers that it could be the former government itself playing god because somebody gave an idiot a little money and gun powder.

When the white man brought the Indian alcohol we destroyed their culture. We destroyed them like we destroyed unwittingly unlike the small pocks laced blankets we gave them. We do things that have dramatic effects on a culture or the landscape without realizing it because we don't prioritize the sanctity of life we instead prioritize power and control. Being the top dog is what America is really all about.

Trump says America 1st…

I say that the planet comes 1st.

There is a difference. If we destroy this World for America we will be left with nothing. All the patriotism in the World can't bring the animals back. The Rhino… the Elephant…

Anything that makes a big trophy for that dentist who is so confused about his education he is still having children swish with a cup of fluoride.

We are so dumb that we are microwaving baby formula when the Russians banned Microwaves in the 1970's.

We are so dumb that we line up single file to give our children autism because we trust the medical establishment.

We are so dumb and psycho that we will crush Libya like it's a game because we are jealous of its gold then in its ruins migrants are being sold as slaves there now

There say there is really no gold in Fort Knocks.

The Fed is resistant to an actual audit or to allow anyone to see if there is even any gold supply in reality backing the currency.

Printed on the Dollar are presidents who would have got rid of the Federal Reserve who prints their faces. They were not spineless.

By overwhelming odds and gruesome slaughter we have made the once fearless and courageous warriors of the natives into spineless drunkards. We destroyed a culture that in many ways is superior to our own with its industrial era and technology.

We still to this day have not learned the importance of the animals over the importance of our money. The Indians drive cars like us when they should still ride horses. They have lost their way and are losing their languages to English. They are losing their culture that was harmonious with nature in exchange for ours where a man looks fat by wearing all the garbage he would have thrown away on his body.

The government shouldn't be involved in Football for instance. Millions are spent to adorn Football with American patriotism but you see on level ground players doing civil protesting the American way...   When Trump says he doesn't like Colin Kaepernick taking a knee he is saying he doesn't like civil protest.

The only alternative to civil protest is a Civil war so why would he be against civil disobedience?

Trump is not thinking this through.

Aside from the redundant police brutality black people are also upset about being targeted racially when it comes to the prison industrial complex.

The star spangled banner has a missing verse black players might not want to stand for when it says "No refuge could save the hireling and slave"

(And where is that band who so vauntingly swore,

That the havoc of war and the battle's confusion

A home and a Country should leave us no more?

Their blood has wash'd out their foul footstep's pollution.

No refuge could save the hireling and slave

From the terror of flight or the gloom of the grave,

And the star-spangled banner in triumph doth wave

O'er the land of the free and the home of the brave.)

In Cascadia taking a knee hits home even more.

Even at Garfield High school players are taking a knee in solidarity. It has reached our children in schools.

Children want to know the dark side of America now because it's been hidden under this mindless waving of the flag.

Thomas Paine said: "The duty of a true Patriot is to protect his country from its government."

In short... a true patriot would be starting a new country like I did in light of all these things.

Washington said we should guard against the impostors of pretend patriotism. If you ask me JFK was the last president who tried to set America back on the right track. He was killed for it.

In the American spirit that Kennedy gave us lives on but must take our own power back as a nation. We can't expect for America to change. We cannot fight with America and win with guns because the US is the best. What we can do is what is proper is solidify a new nation in the west in the name of its better side. In the name of its founders we must secede in the name of all those who believed in true liberty and prosperity.

We must let the land and its rivers and trees and animals come before our national pride. We must let our intellect come before our ego. We must let dying ideas die and remember what is good. We must learn to take care of one another instead of trying to prove who is boss.

Those who are attempting to feed the homeless should no longer be arrested by the former government.

Those who use civil disobedience should not be losing their jobs.

I like what Matt Damon says about Civil disobedience:

"I start from the supposition that the World is topsy-turvy. That things are all wrong. That the wrong people are in jail... and the wrong people are out of jail. That the wrong people are in power and the wrong people are out of power. That the wealth is distributed in this country in such a way as not simply to require small reform, but to require a drastic reallocation of wealth. I start from the supposition that we don't have to say too much about this because all we have to do think about the state of the World today and realize that things are all upside down. Now if you don't think... if you just listen to TV and read scholarly things, you actually begin to think that things are not so bad. Or that just little things are wrong. But you to get a little detached and come back and you are horrified. So we have to start from that supposition that things are really topsy-turvy. And our topic is topsy-turvy... Civil disobedience. Now as soon as you say that the topic is civil disobedience... you are saying that our problem is Civil disobedience. That is not our problem. Our problem is civil obedience. Our problem is that numbers of people all over the World who have obeyed the dictates of the leaders of their government and have gone to war and millions have been killed because of this obedience. We recognize this for Nazi Germany. We know that the problem there was obedience. That the people obeyed Hitler. People obeyed... That was wrong. They should of challenged and they should of resisted! And if we were only there, we would of showed them. Even in Stalin's Russia we can understand that. People were obedient... All these heard like people! Remember those bad old days when people were exploited by feudalism? Everything was terrible in the middle ages. But we now we have western civilization... The rule of law. The rule of law has regularized and maximized the injustice that existed before the rule of law. That is what the rule of law has done. When in all the nations of the World the rule of law is the darling of the leaders and the plague of the people! We ought to begin to recognize this. We have to transcend these national boundaries in our thinking. Nixon and Brezhnev have much more in common with one another than we have with Nixon. J. Edgar

Hoover has more in common with the Soviet secret police than he has with us! It is the international dedication to law and order that binds the leaders of all countries in a comradely bond! That's why we are so surprised when they get together. They smile they shake hands, they smoke cigars. They really like one another no matter what they say. What we are trying to do I assume is really to get back to the principles and aims and spirit of the declaration of independence. This spirit is resistance to illegitimate authority! And to forces that deprive people of their life, liberty and right to pursue happiness...

And therefor under these conditions it urges the right to alter or abolish their current form of government. And the stress had been on "abolish" but to establish the principles of the declaration of independence we're going to need to go outside the law. To stop obeying the laws that demand killing or that allocate wealth the way it's been done... Or that put people in jail for petty technical offenses and keep people out of jail for enormous crimes. My hope is that this kind of spirit will take place not just in this country but in other countries because they all need it. People in all countries need the spirit of disobedience to the state which is not a metaphysical thing, but a thing of force and wealth. And we need a kind of declaration of interdependence among people of all countries of the world who are striving for the same thing."

This speech shows us that not all of our greatest Icons are dead.

It should be written in a book. It should be historical.

Matt Damon is alive with us today saying the same thing.

Civil Disobedience

What is the ultimate in civil disobedience? I will tell you...

It is allot like Eminem holding up a fist after his freestyle about Trump. You can see the same resistance fist on Bernie Sanders.

Sadhu Amar Bharati is an Indian holy man who claims that he has had his right hand raised in the air since 1973. 40 years later, his hand is just a useless piece of skin and bone with thick and twisted nails but he says that Shiva told him to.

He says it is the ultimate symbol of peace and brotherhood.

Let's not forget America shot its greatest civil rights leader Martin Luther King and tried to cover it up. He was a reverend who preached no violence. You can see why the government might be paranoid after shooting him when Black Panthers raise the same fist. The federal government is worried there will be a black uprising to retaliate in light of this. They should be worried.

Martin Luther King would be a good place to say no to the government. No we will not let you kill our greatest icon for racial equality and nonviolence and get away with it. I am saying no here in Cascadia because the government doesn't understand they violated his unalienable right to life.

At what point will you say no?

Will you let them keep building toll roads and a police state till it is too late to say no? It's not too late. I will take the foundation of America with me when I say that I have a right to start a new government. If you try to stop me it will be like Dath Vader thinking he killed Obi-Wan Kenobi. As V said "Ideas are bulletproof." America cannot stop the Cascadian movement.

 Let's just pretend I have the power to physically destroy America with every nation in the World. From every nation that America has ever bombed in history I suddenly have that same power to destroy. That is a vast amount of people. What if I also had the power to reach beyond this book in to physical reality and had the power to even reach Americans themselves…   What if I had all the black people in the World and all the natives at my side?

I become "a threat"

When America sees a threat they use bullets.

They don't care if it's Martin Luther King they are shooting.

They will have a holiday for him and you won't know the difference.

Even the peacemaker may be shot for having too much power.

No one is supposed to have more power than America that is the unwritten rule. America 1st…

America 1st over its own people.

If America put me in a cage would the World get me out?

Perhaps the people have become too spineless. Perhaps all the Indians would rather just drink and all the blacks would turn a blind eye because I am white. If you are a Cascadian you are going to break me out. If you are a Cascadian you are going to care about your president in contrast. I would hope America would want to break Trump out of jail if we locked him up visiting the West coast. You know why? Because man doesn't belong in a cage! I am willing to overlook all America has done.

That is the difference. We aren't looking for revenge even if we have the power to destroy nations. If anything makes Cascadians better than America it is the fact we stick to our guns and we aren't trying escalate conflict because It's not in our bests interests. A family feud can last for generations and that is now what we need in 2017. Americans are our friends and family. They are in our families because they are too stupid to be Cascadians. We accept Americans because we already co-exist.

We aren't afraid of the Muslims because we know how to co-exist. We don't have a travel ban because we aren't afraid of foreign countries like America is. We don't have a border with Mexico because one of my best friends I went through school with was an "illegal immigrant." We are all just people.

The idea that people... can be "illegal" is destroying our bond with friends and families. No one in Cascadia is "illegal" unless they kill someone.

We hold Doug flags on the border with Canada every year I don't see why Cascadians can't expand and do the same thing at the border with Mexico. Maybe all of California is going to be part of Cascadia now. What are you going to do about it America?

The people themselves get to make their own personal decision on this one. I am not forcing them to be Cascadian. I am not overthrowing the American government because Cascadians will do that by their own free will. I don't have to make any orders to do that because I let people decide when they are ready.

Somebody burned down Planned Parenthood for example.

I didn't tell anyone to burn Planned Parenthood they did that of their own free will. I did however say it is banned on the west coast. I don't fight fire with fire.

I want solidarity with the US and I want independence from the US simultaneously. This comes down to Respect.

Americans... they either respect me or they don't.

Cascadians... they either respect me or they don't.

America and Cascadia respect one another and that is what is important. I am not subhuman and I am not a terrorist.

I am a whistleblower and a president.

I am the 1st general of the World ARMY when nations are ready to learn respect for one another.

When there is no World ARMY there is no one at the wheel on Star ship Earth. That is a fact. We are an embarrassment in our leadership globally. No nation wants to back down... they all want to be the top dog.

But that ruffling of feathers...

That scraping of dog feet..

The sabre rattling...

The gloating of military drills to show superiority...

It could be the end of us all if we are not careful as a planet.

It all shows us that the World is out of control.

When the media uses left wing and right wing to divide and conquer us. What is your response?

For the Xennial generation my answer is that we are:

UP,UP

DOWN, DOWN

LEFT RIGHT
LEFT RIGHT

B,A Select Start!

The truth is the founders loathed political parties. A man should represent himself and not be affiliated with groups or political parties.

Jefferson said:

"The greatest good we can do our country is to heal its party divisions and make them one people."

So if you hear that there is a Cascadian party running for office in the US these people have no clue what Cascadia even is or that I left the union in 2014. America will literally likely kill any Cascadian leader that does not have my name. No one will be allowed to leave the union because anyone but me would do it for the wrong reasons without understanding the nation's foundation.

Jefferson said: "If a law is unjust, a man is not only right to disobey it, he is obligated to do so."

Jefferson is so important to Cascadia we have a state of Jefferson in northern California.

We want equality...

We want our right to life to be respected by the government...

If America doesn't understand that we will not be silent forever.

We will eventually take arms from every nation in the World if we have to. It becomes more about awakening the people of planet Earth about the limitations of government across the board. Cascadia will have an influence on every nation for the good of mankind. This influence will come from being on the right side of history not by guns.

The foundation of America isn't crumbling. It is being rebuilt in our Noocracy and future Republic. As we start a new country may it be a learning experience for all Americans instead of another bloody Civil war.

Our children should have a new education that teaches them a multitude of useful vocational careers instead of needless homework to keep them busy. We have been distracted with uselessness for far too long. We have been distracted by our own blind patriotism for far too long.

As time wears on as cowards we lose hope for real change.

In the face of brutality Mahatma Gandhi got people to believe in a non-violent approach so much they were willing to line single file to be beaten. It proves a point but that is not my desire. We just have to have faith that there is still good in the World who are ready to galvanize when our governments have failed us.

Gandhi said: "You must not lose faith in humanity. Humanity is an ocean if a few drops in the ocean are dirty, the ocean does not become dirty.

I have no friends unless all people in the World will be my friend.

I make no divisive separation between people even if I have to make my own country as an oasis for equality.

Civil disobedience starts by staring back into the eyes of the beast. Those what would use others as pawns for their own agendas rather than the good of all have no place in my government. I trust no one with government. I can only trust myself much like you.

Harrison Ford holds a sign that says "Nobody for President" during the last election. Perhaps he understands the feel we have here in the west.

If you become the next great leader every leader in history has already tainted your reputation.

Few were ever great. Few cared about their people more than their own governance. Perhaps it is the nature of man to become so callous. I like to believe otherwise. I have to believe there is benevolence out there I am certain of it.

We have all just been in the back of the room watching the big show. We have been watching as the World slowly destroys its self. If we do nothing and there is no intervention it is certain.

Martin Luther King said "Our lives begin and end the day we become silent about things that matter."

His death matters. I am going to make it matter.

Real civil obedience starts when instead of changing mantras on a blow horn during a protest you tell the police instead:

"You are in the Republic of Cascadia. You are in Cascadian territory. The police of the former US government are ordered to disband. We intend to finally uphold our unalienable right to life! The police are not allowed to shoot our citizens or make barriers. You must disband. You must disperse and leave the area."

Let me tell you right now they aren't going to budge.

America is stubborn and it is stupid.

If a police officer however attempts to arrest someone I suggest you hit them with a paintball gun to mark them. If a police officer from the former government attempts to beat someone I suggest you hit them with a bright yellow paintball gun to warn them. We are not fucking around. These paintballs could be bullets if I decide. America will understand that. America will understand we are not some random rabble but a people who are fed up with police brutality and unnecessary lethal force.

Law enforcement of the former government must respect our unalienable right to life. They must understand that beating people on camera will no longer be tolerated. All it takes is one real Cascadian to wipe out your entire police force.

America should not risk the lives of its officers by continuing to enforce its own laws. We have one law right now America needs to hear about. We have one law right now for America to understand. There is a law against lethal force and execution by the government. Will America learn to obey that law?

How far will you push us? If you do you America will crumble.

The Cascadian Proclamation

We the people of Cascadia and the people of the northwest proclaim for our basic rights and safety a new territory from Jefferson to Alaska. With the consent of the people of British Columbia and Yukon pending a new nation based on our bio-region. For the right of life to be upheld by our government we claim our new destiny to honor all life and set forth a new monument to liberty in the Pacific Northwest. May our trees be protected by the fires that burn with the ego of men. For our waters to run clean undisturbed we unite with new motion to deflect all chaos born from the greed of capitalism... To break from the bonds of currency if they bond us. We proclaim an international sanctuary without fear to protect the wounded of the World. A neutral zone from all war and bloodshed we procure. We laugh at the makers of war and refuse to spoil and uphold their contracts. As the true warriors of peace and children of the rainbow unmatched by fools we walk to uphold our flag. When nationalism is no longer for the benefit of man we forge a new government , unwavering to the demand of more and more needless laws. We are the law. We promise to protect our people from hardships with a new found sensitivity. With our freedom we are bound to our responsibility. We refuse to allow the vindictive to have a voice in justice for the dawn of a golden age without incarceration, torture and punishment. Let there be peace upon our land. And without a drop of blood we leave the union when we are enlightened to the prospect. A foundation for the sons and daughters of man. Without equal, we acknowledge our independence.

The Cascadian Anthem

Where the eagle sheds its wing

where the salmon ride on the Columbia

where the evergreen is king

and the wars of the iron age are under us

Cascadia we'll sing

Cascadia... to Cascadia

our land it must be free

and not the freedom of our past

Where nature turns the road to crumble

Protected by all nations and me.

St. Helens iron mountain make us humble

hold it like a guardian key

Cascadia we'll sing

Cascadia... to Cascadia

our land it must be free

and not the freedom of our past

When the leaders lead the planet into thunder

Where religion is a dangerous thing

When greed has turned the hearts of man to plunder

When the wounded warrior escapes

Cascadia we'll sing

Cascadia... to Cascadia

our land it must be free

and not the freedom of our past

The family of all is great and wonderous

Our mercy is the greatest and peace

Let the stars of the night shine from under us

Like a man with an old kite string

Cascadia we'll sing

Cascadia... to Cascadia

Cascadia we'll sing

Cascadia... to Cascadia

Cascadia we'll sing

Cascadia... to Cascadia

For all!

This book is dedicated to all the truth seekers and rabble rousers...

All the misfits who went AWOL in a fraud war...

All the veteran suicides...

People like Cindy Sheehan and Jacob Jefferson Brisbine!

Banksy street art...

John Lennon and Yoko Ono

All the victims of 9-11 and John Stewart.

All the firefighters who fight menacing fires...

A number of US presidents who were rolling in their graves

Martin Luther King

Bruce Lee

Jimmi Hendrix

Mahatma Gandhi

Kurt Kobain

Chris Cornell

Muhammad Ali

Jane Goodall and all the animals that need to be saved...

The Pleadians from planet Erra and the Light forms!

Stanislav Petrov because he could of blown us up but he didn't.

"I've wrestled with alligators I've tussled with a whale. I've done handcuffed lightning and thrown thunder in jail. You know I'm bad. Just last week, I murdered a rock, I injured a stone, Hospitalized a brick, I'm so mean I make medicine sick." –Muhammad Ali

Well medicine is sick... And it's time to handcuff lightning.

Keep your hate in America everybody. Let us have our own cloud. America can't make you fight if you don't want to.

"I got nothing against no Viet cong. No Vietnamese ever called me a Nigger."

Refuse to let people and governments to walk all over you.

Be like Muhammad Ali...

Refuse to fight in Vietnam.

Break him out if they put him in jail for it.

Be like Wesley Snipes

Refuse to pay taxes.

Refuse their kangaroo courts on the west coast because America doesn't understand basic rights yet.

Refuse to let America lock people up.

Refuse to let America execute people.

Refuse to let the cops blow people away.

WEST

COAST

DON'T

FUCK

WITH!